Democratic Souvenirs

Democratic Souvenirs

An Historical Anthology of
19th - century American Music

Selected, with Introduction and Commentary, by
RICHARD JACKSON
Head, Americana Collection, Music Division
The New York Public Library

Foreword by Virgil Thomson

The Americana Collection Music Series: Number Three

Published for The New York Public Library by
C. F. PETERS CORPORATION
NEW YORK   LONDON   FRANKFURT

The title of this anthology is after the title of
Walt Whitman's poem *Souvenirs of Democracy*.

The frontispiece is from the cover of the sheet music of
Thomas Baker's *The Sparkling Polka* (New York: Horace
Waters, 1855). To quote *Early American Sheet Music* (New York:
Bowker, 1941), "The two floors of the Horace
Waters store are shown: the piano 'saloon' above, and the
music 'saloon' below" (p. 91). Lithograph by Sarony & Co.

The cover design is from the cover of the songster
Songs from O'Malley ([Philadelphia] Godey & M'Michael
[c1842]).

Copyright © 1988 by C. F. Peters Corporation, New York

Typographical errors in the musical text have been corrected
and editorial suggestions added wherever possible.

Designed by Marilan Lund

Library of Congress Cataloging-in-Publication Data
Democratic souvenirs.
(The Americana Collection music series; no. 3)
Reprints of 37 compositions: songs, piano pieces,
excerpts from theatrical works, hymns, choruses,
chamber music, and orchestral music.
Bibliography: p.
Includes index.
1. Music—United States—19th century—Scores.
I. Jackson, Richard, 1936–   II. Series.
M1495.D36   1987   87-754134
ISBN 0-938856-03-0

Dedicated to
Vera Brodsky Lawrence
with affection and appreciation

Table of Contents

Foreword, by Virgil Thomson	ix
Introduction, by Richard Jackson	xi

THE MUSIC
(arranged chronologically in each section by copyright date)

I. SONGS

Mary's Tears, by Oliver Shaw	3
The Ocean, by Edward L. White	5
May I Hope to Call Thee Friend, by James M. Deems	7
Love's Call'd a Dream, by Asahel Abbott	10
Uncle Tom's Cabin, by W. J. Wetmore	14
The Fountain, by Lucien H. Southard	17
Rosalie, the Prairie Flower, by George F. Root	23
Break, Break, Break, by Alfred H. Pease	26
The Sea, by Edward MacDowell	30
The Stars and Stripes Forever, by John Philip Sousa	32

II. PIANO PIECES

The Wood Pigeon, by George Dutton, Jr.	39
The Will o' the Wisp, by George William Warren	44
Souvenir de Porto Rico, by Louis Moreau Gottschalk	49
Crystal Spring: Tremolo, by Stephen A. Emery	60
Silver Spring, by William Mason	64
Annie and I, by Ellsworth C. Phelps	78
Maple Leaf Rag, by Scott Joplin	85

III. THEATRICAL MUSIC

Jim Crow	91
Ole Dan Tucker	94
Farewell Ladies, by E. P. Christy	98
Oh! Susanna, by Stephen Foster	102
Notre-Dame of Paris: Act I, no. 8, by William Henry Fry	105

Evangeline: "Golden Chains," by Edward E. Rice	117
Rip Van Winkle: "Who are all these folks I see?" by George F. Bristow	124
Azara: Act II, Scene V (vocal score), by John Knowles Paine	132

IV. CHORAL MUSIC
(Anthems, Glees, Hymns, Oratorios)

Bee's Wings & Fish, by Henry Dielman	157
Hymn for Whitsunday, by Peter Erben	159
Safely thro' Another Week, by Lowell Mason	161
Endymion, by George Henry Curtis	162
Praise Ye the Lord, by Ambrose Davenport	166
Three Kings of Orient, by John Henry Hopkins, Jr.	177
St. Peter: nos. 34 and 35, by John Knowles Paine	178
Rock of Ages, by Dudley Buck	188

V. CHAMBER MUSIC

Pensées musicales (movement VI: "Bolero"), by Charles C. Perkins	195
Allegro de Concert (Quartette for Saxophones), by Caryl Florio	202

VI. ORCHESTRA MUSIC

Piano Concerto (last movement: *allegro con scioltezza*), by Amy Marcy Cheney Beach	227
Jubilee (Symphonic Sketches: I), by George W. Chadwick	252

Biographical Sketches	291
Appendix I: Alphabetical Listing of Works with Bibliographical Sources	334
Appendix II: Index of Composers	335

Foreword

ANY MUSIC distributed in the Americas during colonial times—Spanish, French, or British—was virtually all of it either a direct import or a simplified local version of some European model. It was only after political emancipation had been achieved that the artistic holds of Europe began to loosen. By the end of World War I, when the United States had become a world power, U.S. music, also quite perceptibly that of Mexico and Brazil, had begun to swim in wider waters, sometimes even as far as to Europe itself.

It was during the century and a quarter between our political independence and our coming to Europe's military rescue in 1917 that a sort of adolescence had taken place, with all the growing pains and emotional uncertainties of that uneasy passage. From the charming stiffnesses of the Federal style in music (for Presidential ceremonies and social dancing) through the operatic melodramas that were essayed both sides of mid-century, along with the popular success of phony "coon songs" and of a more nearly authentic, in any case highly polished Negro minstrelsy, to the utter sophistication all-round, both musical and sociological, of ragtime and blues, our 19th century toward its end facilitated full maturation in the classical techniques for John Knowles Paine and Edward MacDowell, as well as the eclosion of de Koven and Victor Herbert as masters of light opera. The latter phenomenon, along with black jazz, preceded, right after World War I, a take-over by English-speaking America of a major share in the international pop trade, and of the rest of it by Latins from Cuba, Brazil, and Mexico.

It was about that time, too, that we began to export, instead of merely to import, classical music in all the current styles, along with performing artists and pedagogues, many of them locally trained, and musical instruments locally manufactured. These achievements mark the beginning of our first real "take-off" fully airborne, an operation still far from being a take-over comparable in power to our accomplishments in poetry, fiction, and oil-painting. But it was a musical coming-out that we can realize had been preparing itself for over a hundred years.

And we can now pretty clearly see as inevitable that we should start making known and available certain delicious moments and the still handsome relics of our youth. They are in our libraries. So it is our libraries' privilege, with help from our music publishers, to get them around.

Richard Jackson, of The New York Public Library, has long served many of us individually as a keybearer to all this wealth. Now he is opening the door wider, as are indeed the many collectors and scholars now busy across our land at trying to arrest the erosion of our musical mementos. This is not the first effort of its kind. But it is timely service to the avid interest in our music and its growing-up that is already an ongoing concern of the musical community, not only at home but also abroad and in the other Americas.

VIRGIL THOMSON

Introduction

> After all, not to create only, or found only,
> But to bring, perhaps from afar, what is already founded,
> To give it our own identity, average, limitless, free...
> To obey, as well as command—to follow, more than to lead;
> These also are the lessons of our New World;
> —While how little the New, after all, how much the
>   Old, Old World!
>
>   WALT WHITMAN
>   *Song of the Exposition* (1871)

> True, it may be said, the emotional, moral and aesthetic natures of humanity have not radically changed—that in these the old poems apply to our times and all times, irrespective of date; and that they are of incalculable value as pictures of the past.
>   WALT WHITMAN
>   *A Backward Glance o'er Travel'd Roads* (1888)

Many American "music lovers" seem to love 19th-century European classical music. To the exclusion of American music. They love some 18th-century European music and some early 20th-century European music, to be sure. But mostly 19th century. And why not? It can be so grand, so soothing, so melodious, so romantic, so delightful, so colorful, so sonorous, so sad, so happy, so moving in general, so learned, so involved, so simple, so profound, so analogous to the human situation—so beautiful. Certainly, some of these works are among the glories of Western civilization. Much of the music is the bread and butter of most of our opera and ballet companies, of our concert and recital halls, of our recording companies (if they record classical music at all). This is what the majority of audiences seem to want and this is what they get.

If one doubts the truth of the preponderance of European repertory among the large U.S. musical performance organizations, books such as the following should be consulted:

Arthur Bloomfield. *The San Francisco Opera: 1922–1978.* Sausalito, Cal.: Comstock Editions, 1978.

Lincoln Kirstein. *Thirty Years: Lincoln Kirstein's The New York City Ballet.* 2nd ed. New York: Knopf, 1978.

Kate Hevner Mueller. *Twenty-seven Major American Symphony Orchestras: A History and Analysis of Their Repertories, Seasons 1842–43 through 1969–70.* Bloomington: Indiana University Studies, 1973.

William H. Seltsam. *Metropolitan Opera Annals: A Chronicle of Artists and Performances.* New York: The H. W. Wilson Co., 1947.

    First Supplement: 1947–1957. New York: The H. W. Wilson Co., 1957.

    Second Supplement: 1957–1966. New York: The H. W. Wilson Co., 1968.

    Third Supplement: 1966–1976. Clifton, N.J.: James T. White & Co., 1978.

Martin L. Sokol. *The New York City Opera: An American Adventure.* [p. 215]: *Annals of the New York City Opera 1944–1981*, compiled by George Louis Mayer (through 1979) and Martin L. Sokol (1980 and 1981). New York: Macmillan Pub. Co., 1981.

The program managers of many "good" music radio stations are careful to broadcast mostly 19th-century

INTRODUCTION

European music, from the masterworks to the obscure and artistically suspicious. (The most chic of these stations *do*, however, broadcast much 18th-century European music.) The patrons will be pleased, the sponsors will be pleased. Oh, there may be a non-European work now and then, and perhaps on the Fourth of July American music might dominate. Otherwise, the standard fare is European.

It was more understandable, if indeed misguided, for 19th-century Americans, especially *early* 19th-century Americans, to adopt and promote European music. There wasn't a great deal of the native product around in the early years of that century, after all. But it is scandalous for such a situation to exist today. Historians have long pointed out the inferiority complex in artistic matters of the United States. Yet this fearful American adoption of European art, especially music, continues in a grand way.

Yet, as is true of many arts and of the sciences, music is multifaceted. The expression "world of music" is commonplace. And while the concept of "world" may be a bit too broad to describe it in actuality, the field of music does encompass a wide variety of activities. It can embrace, say, the collecting of marches exclusively on LP records, the study of the organ-grinder repertory in five Italian cities in the 1890s, the taking of tap-dance lessons, the performance of contemporary Polish chamber music, membership in a rock group, membership in a church choir, rabid devotion to and connoisseurship of Broadway musicals of the 1920s, the composition of advertising jingles for a cigarette company, etc. The field is at least as broad as that of, say, American Studies (as discussed by Stuart Levine in the Sonneck Society *Newsletter* 8 [Fall 1982], 53–56).

But in the eyes of many otherwise intelligent and rational people, to be involved in music—especially for a "cultivated" person—somehow means to be involved in European music (largely 19th-century). And this idea holds sway more than two hundred years after the U.S.A. became a name and declared independence! It seems that a colonial mentality is difficult to shake off entirely.

"Information [abroad] regarding musical conditions in America is in the same state as information regarding literary conditions [was] fifty years ago.... There are even now persons in Europe pretending high culture who, if they should visit Detroit, would expect to find Indians and buffalo roaming on Woodward or Jefferson avenues.... Can any good music come from American composers? My answer to foreigners is, come and see." These remarks were made in 1914 (by Francis L. York in an article entitled "Foreign Ignorance of American Music" on page 30 of the April 18th issue of the magazine *Musical America*). They might have been made today, for the conditions they describe remain all too true. Since most Americans know little of their own historical concert music (the field of *contemporary* popular music is perhaps different)—or *contemporary* concert music for that matter—they do not speak or write of it abroad, publicize it abroad, or perform it abroad. (They do not do these things with any great frequency in the U.S.A. either.) Not that some of this music has not been performed abroad. It was and is, but only sporadically. No extended tradition of performing this music exists in any country in the world. As Virgil Thomson has written: "Everywhere our jazz and pop are respected, but not so our symphonic and opera creations, our chamber music and our lieder" (*A Virgil Thomson Reader*. Boston: Houghton Mifflin Co., 1981; p. [406]).

Mr. York, who was president of the Detroit Conservatory of Music at the time (1914), also notes in the same article that "one thing that has made it difficult for the American composer to obtain a hearing is the fact that until recently nearly all of our conductors of orchestras and operas have been foreign. Naturally they are much more acquainted with standard authors as Beethoven or Mendelssohn than with the new compositions of the American John Smith or Henry Jones." (Or with their *old* compositions, one might add.) Fortunately, this situation has changed somewhat, but as a matter of fact, whenever American concert works and non-standard European works have been programmed (when at all) over the past seventy or eighty years, they have been referred to by many musicians, listeners, and critics as "novelties."

This situation has been aggravated, perhaps, by the large influx of foreign musicians in general over the decades of the 19th and 20th centuries, not only as visitors on tour but also as immigrants. For instance, of the nineteen professional groups of arriving immigrants for 1879 mentioned by the *American Art Journal* in its issue of January 29, 1881 (p. 272), the largest was musicians (it numbered 341).

INTRODUCTION

The love affair—a terribly one-sided one, in fact—is stultifying, gloomy, and unhealthy. The situation should be altered. The object of the affection is in no danger if its profile is lowered somewhat. The lover should be shaken (gently, if possible) to his or her senses and provided with an attractive alternative. All three could become the best of friends.

The shaking to sense of the lover could come ideally through education, of course. As Arnold Rosen of Warner Bros. Music observed in the December 1982 *Music Publishers Association Newsletter*: "The serious [or "classical"] music market is affected by higher costs and less income, but most of all by the continued failure of the educational system to teach an appreciation of our cultural heritage and its art forms." And this education should perhaps be a little more objective than it usually is, slightly detached and not so attuned to (always predominantly non-American) masterpieces. Traditionally, the manner in which music history courses—and many other music courses (including training in individual performance, in fact)—has been conducted is for a (usually harried, indifferent, or superior-acting) teacher to unveil a limited series of works which one is supposed to know. (This, of course, also occurs in art history classes and in other disciplines.) These works are invariably European, many from the 19th century. By this means, one is supposed to "know" the art.

This manner has had its detractors. Arthur Shepherd, an experienced composer-conductor who worked for years in Cleveland, asked the Music Teachers National Association in 1947: "Why should not classes . . . be required to memorize themes from American symphonies, sonatas, chamber music, operas as well as from traditional masterpieces?" (Shepherd, p. 35). (If there was an answer, it has not been found by me.)

Why not indeed, Mr. Shepherd? Because a knowledge of past European music is considered far more important than a knowledge of past American music. Those of us who have received a music education in this country have probably been introduced, in one way or another, to a few European pinnacles of the art, while so-called lesser European works and American works of whatever "quality" are dismissed if they are mentioned at all. By not taking a more socially oriented, a more socially aware route, this education has been terribly faulty. As Tom Wolfe has quite rightly said: "To [the educated classes], great ideas come from the cosmos. It's impossible for a devotee of this world to approach art in a sociological fashion—to see that styles change for reasons of fashion, just as they do in other worlds" (quoted in Schwartz, p. 58).

Just as in the present century, America produced in the 19th century much popular music as well as classical music. In fact, there are those who think that, in general, popular music was more vigorous and dominant here for most of that century (see "American Democracy and American Music" in Lowens). Some of this popular music is especially piquant and unexpectedly has had echoes across the decades. Some was simply very much of its time and place (such as the Root and Wetmore pieces reprinted here). Several examples of popular music are included in this anthology because of the major role that this music played in the daily lives of so many 19th-century Americans.

About the last century's concert music, of which 20th-century musicians and audiences know so little, the general opinion is very low. The Britisher Wilfrid Mellers stated a typical opinion in his *Music in a New Found Land*:

> In nineteenth-century America there was . . . no dearth of deadly serious composers bent on revealing as much soul as they were capable of: only the music that came out, however honourably intended and technically proficient, proved to be mostly an academic exercise in a European idiom. . . . the massive scores have mouldered on the shelves of libraries. (New York: Knopf, 1965; p. 244)

And Frank Rossiter, the brilliant biographer of Charles Ives, wrote in his otherwise fine article, "The 'Genteel Tradition' in American Music":

> these [composers] were the earliest generations in which considerable numbers . . . were trained in Europe. . . . They knew they could not live up to the high standards of Europe in their own compositions—but they could certainly try. (*Journal of American Culture* 4:4 [Winter 1981], p. 108)

In the same article Rossiter also mentions that these composers tended to have a "genteel philosophy" and that they were "burdened by a cultural inferiority complex" (p. 108).

xiii

INTRODUCTION

"Honourably intended," "technically proficient," "European idiom," "genteel"—yes, these are the terms which have perhaps been heard most often in the litany that has arisen among critics in the last thirty years or so in their pejorative descriptions of 19th-century American concert music. With apologies to the distinguished musicologist Joseph Kerman (see his article "A Profile for American Musicology"), I would suggest that a solely critical approach to the study of music history has produced the above terms and that such an approach is wrong.

We may not *like* all of the music of the last century (and one should not feel, anyway, that one must merely *like* a person or a piece to study it or help restore it to history), but we cannot, like ostriches, bury our heads and pretend it does not exist. Neither should we attempt to measure the artifacts and artistic opinions of another era using philosophical yardsticks only recently fashioned. I have attempted in this anthology—and there could, of course, be more than one—to give a view of the kinds of music that were produced in the United States during the 19th century. Some of this music we might consider "good," some of it not so "good." Nevertheless, all of it was composed, used, and heard here.

My criterion for including a certain composer or composition was twofold: 1) There were certain names, by reason of their importance then, that I felt could not be omitted—names like Gottschalk, Foster, Shaw, Beach, Sousa, Joplin, Bristow, Paine, Buck, the two Masons, Fry, Warren, and Root. Then, too, there were certain compositions which, I felt, must be included—compositions such as Chadwick's *Jubilee,* Phelps's *Annie and I,* an excerpt from Rice's *Evangeline,* the lovely chorus "Farewell Ladies." 2) All composers had to be American-born. (The two exceptions to this little rule, Caryl Florio [real name: William James Robjohn], who was born in England, and Henry Dielman, a native of Germany, came to the United States in their teens. Their entire artistic output was made in this country. I could not possibly omit them—such typical American musicians of their day—simply because they happened to be born in other countries.)

The word "historical" appears in the subtitle of this anthology. Yet among the contents are compositions that immediately could be considered as major works of their composers' and within the picture of 19th-century American music—and for today. (And I have used the adjective "American" here and in the subtitle only for convenience; it is intended to signify "of the United States" only, not of the other countries on the American continent. Such usage is not really accurate but it has a venerable history.) Certainly Gottschalk's *Souvenir de Porto Rico* is a classic, a jewel. So, too, is Sousa's *Stars and Stripes Forever,* though the less familiar song version of that piece appears here. Foster's delightful "Oh! Susanna" is easily a classic in its way, as is the quirky and ubiquitous "Ole Dan Tucker." High up with some of their other symphonic contemporaries are Chadwick's *Jubilee* and Mrs. Beach's fine piano concerto, two works that would be superior in the music of any country, yet both so American.

Then there are pieces here that have been used and heard so often that few people think of them as part of 19th-century American music, pieces such as Lowell Mason's sturdy hymn "Safely thro' Another Week" and John Hopkins' beguiling "Three Kings of Orient."

And few of us have not heard and perhaps marvelled at *Maple Leaf Rag,* even if we didn't know the title or that Scott Joplin was its incredibly gifted composer or that it was composed in 1897 and published in 1899.

This anthology also contains several pieces that are outstanding but which, for some unfortunate reason or reasons, are not widely known. Among these certainly are the two excerpts by John Knowles Paine, a great figure but one curiously and unjustly neglected,* and the thoughtful, musicianly anthem by Dudley Buck, an expert though generally ignored composer.

Biographical Sketches

The biographical sketches are generally in inverse proportion to the amount of accurate information available elsewhere on each person: the more accurate information available, the shorter the sketch. In these cases, I have tried to indicate one or more unusual or previously little-touched sources. I have

---

*For instance, the performance of Paine's *Symphony No. 2* by the New York Philharmonic in November 1986 was apparently only the second time that any work of his was given by that organization (see Mueller's *Twenty-seven Major American Symphony Orchestras,* cited earlier).

not, for example, made references to the readily available *The New Grove Dictionary of American Music* (1986), which came out while this work was going through the press. The sketches are fuller, however, where I have felt the subject has been somewhat slighted by "musicologists" (Sousa, for instance) or where information on dates and events is scattered (Buck, for instance). The same is true where extensive information on a subject is available only in fairly obscure and difficult to obtain sources (Deems, for instance). Then, too, even the existing writings on some of the better-known musical figures are shot through with mistakes. The diligent researcher must be ever vigilant to separate fact from error and fiction.

The sketches on Davenport, Dutton, and Erben, in particular, are relatively brief, not because there is a quantity of accurate information available on these men and their works. Just the opposite. I could find little about them. They were not widely famous in their day—typical as they perhaps were—and hence, coldheartedly, were unsung then and now. Thanks largely to the lopsided concerns of American musicology, many lives have faded from music history.

Considering the sketches in the aggregate, Louis Moreau Gottschalk seems to emerge as the dominant figure. And this is perhaps an accurate mirror of his times, for Gottschalk was something of a brilliant star around which all the lesser lights seemed to revolve. He touched the worlds of the "popular" and the "classical" and triumphed in both. He touched the lives of many other performers and composers, and that touch was indelible.

It is hoped that others will take up the few "leads" I have uncovered on the most obscure composers in this anthology. Not that there are not others in our past or present who might be considered interesting or worthy of study. There are many others. In any case, in writing the biographical sketches I have striven for accuracy above all else. And so for any factual lapses I apologize to all the men and women whose words and music make up this anthology, and to the reader.

Bibliographies and Notes

A guide to much information published prior to 1939 on the composers here is available in the *Bio-bibliographical Index of Musicians in the United States since Colonial Times* (Washington, D.C.: Music Section, Pan American Union, 1941; reprinted NY: Da Capo, 1971). I have drawn on these references freely in compiling the biographical sketches and have listed references to books, articles, letters, and dissertations that are not necessarily included in the *Bio-bibliographical Index* which have proved especially useful in compiling the sketches, which have been mentioned in the sketches, or which simply supplement the *Bio-bibliographical Index*. I have not included references here to all known information in published sources.

Citations for many books and newspaper and magazine articles are included in the body of each sketch (usually with abbreviated references to the bibliography at the end of each sketch). Only two or three "informational" footnotes are used, and these are noted with an asterisk (*). There are no numbered notes either at the foot of pages or in a separate section. There is a smattering of duplicate citations in the sketch and its appended bibliography, though never exact duplications. *All* quotations are sourced.

Illustrations

A statement about, and apology for, the illustrations should be made. Many of them are of very poor quality because they have come from a wide range of sources. And even in the cases where separate prints were used—as opposed to reproductions from old books, etc.—these were often flawed and murky. Nevertheless, all were included because of their rarity and intrinsic interest. If not identified otherwise, all illustrations are from the Iconography collection in the Music Division of The New York Public Library.

Acknowledgements

I owe an enormous debt of gratitude to various officials of The New York Public Library, primarily Frank C. Campbell, retired Chief of the Music Division, and Ruth Ann Stewart, formerly Associate Director of External Services, who were most enthusiastic, supportive, and totally cooperative during the preparation of this work. Also helpful and attentive were William L. Coakley, the Library's Managing Editor, Marilan M. Lund, Coordinator of the Graphics Office, and Jean Bowen, who was Assistant Chief of the Music Division when this anthology was assembled and who is now that division's Chief. Among these officials, too, were the energetic and hardwork-

INTRODUCTION

ing President of the Library, Vartan Gregorian, and the knowledgeable David H. Stam, former Andrew W. Mellon Director of The Research Libraries.

Heartfelt thanks to that ebullient composer and man of letters Virgil Thomson for his generous and charming Foreword to this collection.

I am especially grateful to Vera Brodsky Lawrence, the dedicatee of this volume. She has been so generous with her time, knowledge, and general expertise. She has also read specific biographical sketches I had written for inclusion in this book and caught several terrible factual errors which were calmly masquerading as gospel truths. Dear Vera, thanks for your numerous kindnesses to me!

I certainly will never forget those others—authorities on the lives and careers of certain individuals—who willingly read drafts of biographical sketches and made such valuable criticisms, corrections, and suggestions—always being careful of my feelings. The world of music scholarship is richer for their contributions, and I am saved from many embarrassing mistakes. These others are Adrienne Fried Block, Polly Carder, Frank J. Cipolla, Bruce N. Degen, Kenneth Graber, Margery Morgan Lowens, and Deane L. Root. While extending my warmest gratitude to these seven scholars, I, of course, accept the responsibility for any errors that might have crept in.

Special thanks to my good friend Don Gillespie, who is Director of Special Editorial Projects and a Vice President of C. F. Peters Corporation, to Stephen Fisher, the President of that company, and to the charming Mrs. Walter Hinrichsen, Chairman of the Board.

For acts of kindness and thoughtfulness, and for the occasional extraordinary "tip," I would also like to thank Karen Beckers, Mary Jane Corry, Thurston Dox (who helped me in several ways), Donald L. Hixon, Charles Kuralt, Robert Offergeld, Neil Ratliff, Joseph Ruffino, Brooks Shepard, Jr., Bruce Wilson, and especially Dora J. Wilson.

For searching items of information or material for me, my heartfelt thanks to Cathy S. Balshone (Boston Conservatory of Music), Ruth Bleeker (Boston Public Library), Sara J. Clarke (New York State Historical Association), Theresa-Ann Cuda (Utica, N.Y., Public Library), John Cushing (Massachusetts Historical Society), Mary Wallace Davidson (Sibley Library, Eastman School of Music), Huib Deetman (Openbare Bibliotheek, Amsterdam, The Netherlands), John G. Doyle, Carol Emrich (Local History Division, Rochester Public Library), David Kelleher, Thomas J. Kenny (Brooklyn Public Library), Claire M. Lamers (Brooklyn Historical Society), Frank K. Lorenz (Hamilton College), Michael Ochs (Loeb Library, Harvard University), Geraldine Ostrove (Music Division, Library of Congress), Natalie Palme (The Harvard Musical Association), Elizabeth Pattengill (Utica, N.Y., Public Library), Douglas M. Preston (The Oneida Historical Society), Hester Rich (Library of The Maryland Historical Society), Matthew J. Simon (Chief Librarian, Queens College, the City University of New York), and Fritz W. Zwart (Music Dept./Archives, Haags Gemeentemuseum, Gravenshage, The Netherlands).

For answering questions or hauling out heavy volumes, my appreciation to members of the library staffs of the American Antiquarian Society, the New-York Historical Society, and the Peabody Conservatory of Music.

I especially wish to acknowledge my deep gratitude to my sharp and indefatigable typist, Tema Hecht, and researcher, Ann Berent.

Finally, I take this opportunity to thank David P. McKay whose idea it was so long ago that I put together an anthology of 19th-century American music.

Bibliography

Kerman, Joseph. "A Profile for American Musicology." *Journal of the American Musicological Society* 18 (1965), 61.

Lowens, Irving. *Music and Musicians in Early America*. New York: Norton, 1964.

Schwartz, Tony. "Tom Wolfe: The Great Gadfly." *The New York Times Magazine*, Dec. 20, 1981.

Shepherd, Arthur. "American Music in the Limelight," in *Volume of Proceedings of the Music Teachers National Association*. Forty-first series. Seventy-fifth year. Theodore Finney, ed. Pittsburgh: Published by the Association, 1947.

RICHARD JACKSON

The Music

I. Songs

MARY'S TEARS.

A Favorite Song,

FROM MOORE'S SACRED MELODIES, com. by

O. Shaw.

Sung at the Oratorio performed by the HANDEL & HAYDN SOCIETY, in Boston, July 5th 1817, in presence of the PRESIDENT OF THE UNITED STATES.

Third Edition.

PROVIDENCE, Published and sold by the AUTHOR No. 70 Westminster St.

LARGHETTO

Were not the sin—ful Ma—ry's tears An off'—ring wor—thy heav'n, An off'—ring wor—thy heav'n,

Entered according to Act of Congress, the Fourth day of December 1828.

2.

When, bringing every balmy sweet
Her day of luxury stor'd,
She o'er her Saviour's hallow'd feet
The precious perfume pour'd,—

3.

And wip'd them with that golden hair,
Where once the diamond shone,
Though now those gems of grief were there,
Which shine for God alone!

4.

Thou that hast slept in error's sleep,
Oh! would'st thou wake in heaven,
Like Mary kneel, like Mary weep,
"Love much," and be forgiven!

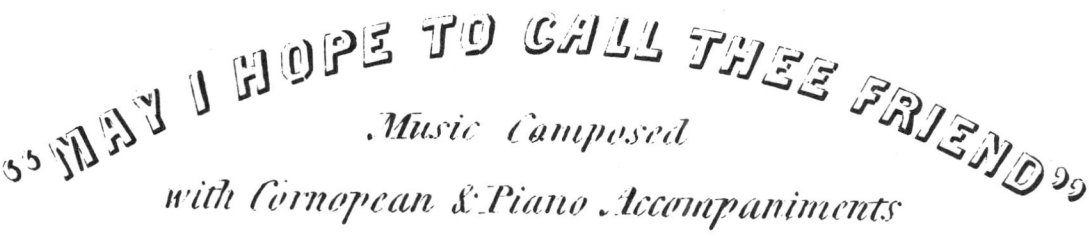

"MAY I HOPE TO CALL THEE FRIEND"

Music Composed

with Cornopean & Piano Accompaniments

And Respectfully Dedicated to

MISS CAROLINE V. CESSNA

(of Cumberland Md.)

BY

JAMES M. DEEMS.

Baltimore, Published by G. Willig Jr.

Andante affetuoso.

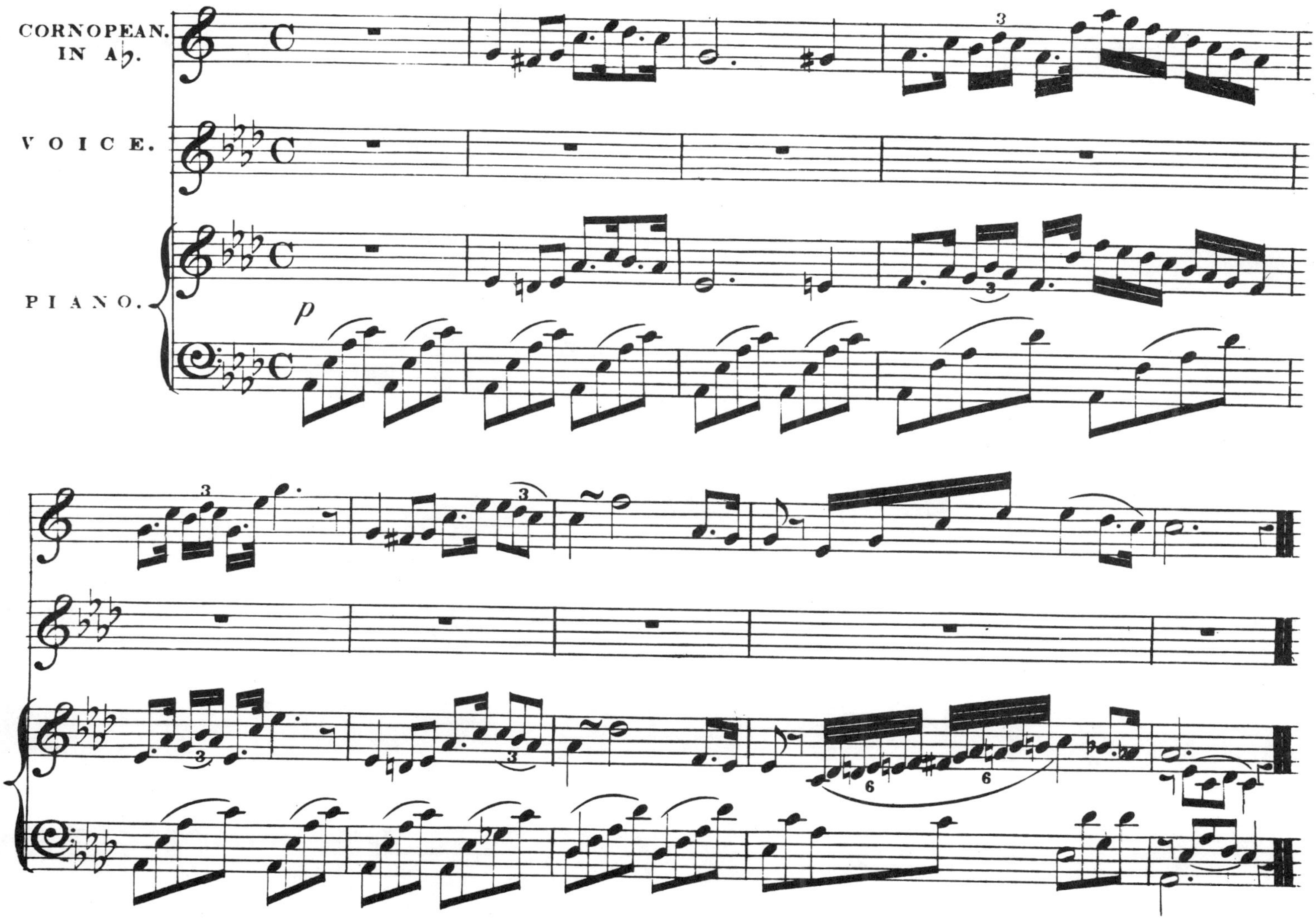

8 · *May I Hope to Call Thee Friend*

2.

Should scandal with envenomed tongue
    Attempt to reach thine ear,
And by false means to do me wrong,
    May kindly trust be near.
Believe, then, through my after life
    My cherished pride shall be,
In joy, or grief, or gladness rife,
    To prize a friend in thee!

LOVE'S CALL'D A DREAM.

Love's Call'd a Dream · 11

12 · *Love's Call'd a Dream*

3

Then let me still love on and sleep,
    With visions thus serene,
'Twere sweeter than to wake and weep
    At such a heartless scene,
As this bright world with all its bloom,
    In all its rich hues drest,
Without a charm to light our gloom,
    Or set the heart at rest.

UNCLE TOM'S CABIN.

WRITTEN AND ARRANGED BY W.J. WETMORE ESQ.R

Uncle Tom's Cabin · 15

2
Oh! how my heart for my fond ones was beating,
   Each claim'd the love a fathers heart knew well;
We had no care — for happy was our meeting,
   Why should we ever know a sad farewell!
         I'll never leave thee, ne'er will I roam,
         Oh! how I love my own dear Cabin Home.

3
Oft round the door when stars were shining brightly,
   Happy we pass'd the summers evening hours;
We play'd the banjo, sung and tripp'd it lightly,
   Over the green bedeck'd with sweetest flowers.
         I'll never leave thee, ne'er will I roam,
         Oh! how I love my own dear Cabin Home.

4
Gaily we danced when e'er the banjo tumming,
   Fill'd every heart with pleasure and delight;
Loudly we heard the old tambo a drumming,
   And every heart pass'd merrily the night.
         I'll never leave thee, ne'er will I roam,
         Oh! how I love my own dear Cabin Home.

5
I now am old but o'er the Past I ponder,
   Happy to see the sports I loved of yore;
Through the bananna groves I love to wander,
   Sad that they'll soon wave over me no more!
         I'll never leave thee, ne'er will I roam,
         Oh! how I love my own dear Cabin Home.

(Swain Engr)

THE FOUNTAIN.

L. H. SOUTHARD.

18 · The Fountain

20 · *The Fountain*

22 · *The Fountain*

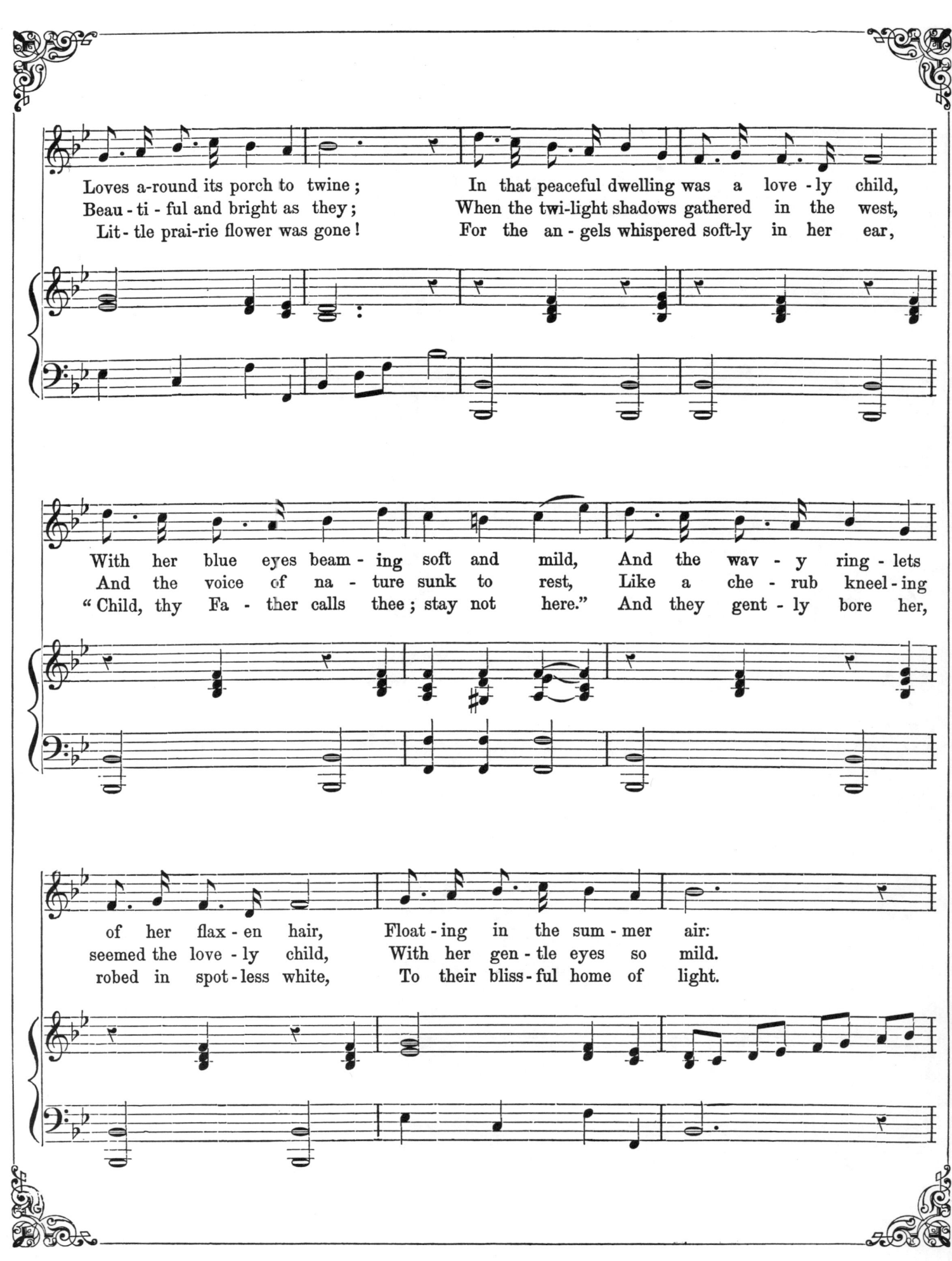

To Mrs. J. V. N. YATES.
Cleveland Ohio.

"BREAK, BREAK, BREAK"

Words by TENNYSON.   Music by ALFRED H. PEASE.

Break, Break, Break · 27

The Sea.
Das Meer.

The Stars and Stripes Forever.
SONG.

Words and Music by JOHN PHILIP SOUSA.

II. Piano Pieces

40 · The Wood Pigeon

42 · *The Wood Pigeon*

The Wood Pigeon · 43

THE WILL O' THE WISP

GEORGE W. WARREN.

46 · The Will o' the Wisp

The Will o' the Wisp · 47

48 · The Will o' the Wisp

A Mr ERNEST LUBECK

Souvenir de Porto Rico

Marche des Gibaros

pour

PIANO

par

L. M. GOTTSCHALK

OP. 31.

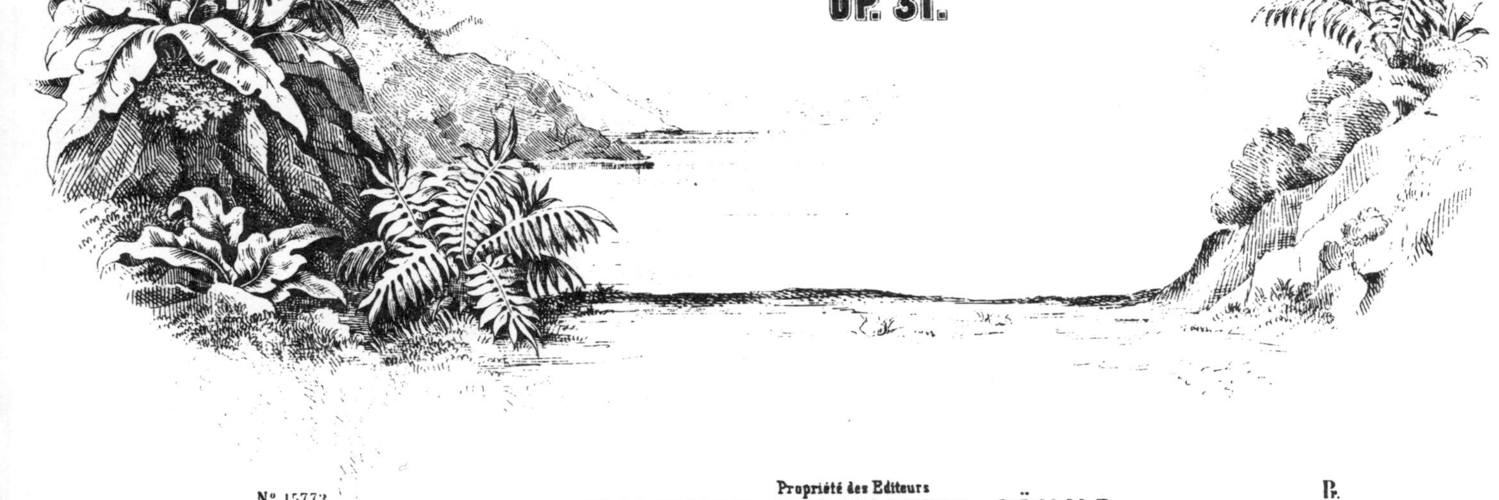

No 15773.

Propriété des Editeurs

MAYENCE, B. SCHOTT'S SÖHNE

Londres, Schott & Co.
159 Regent Street

Bruxelles, Schott frères
82 Montagne de la Cour

P.

SOUVENIR DE PORTO RICO.

MARCHE DES GIBAROS L. M. GOTTSCHALK Op. 31.

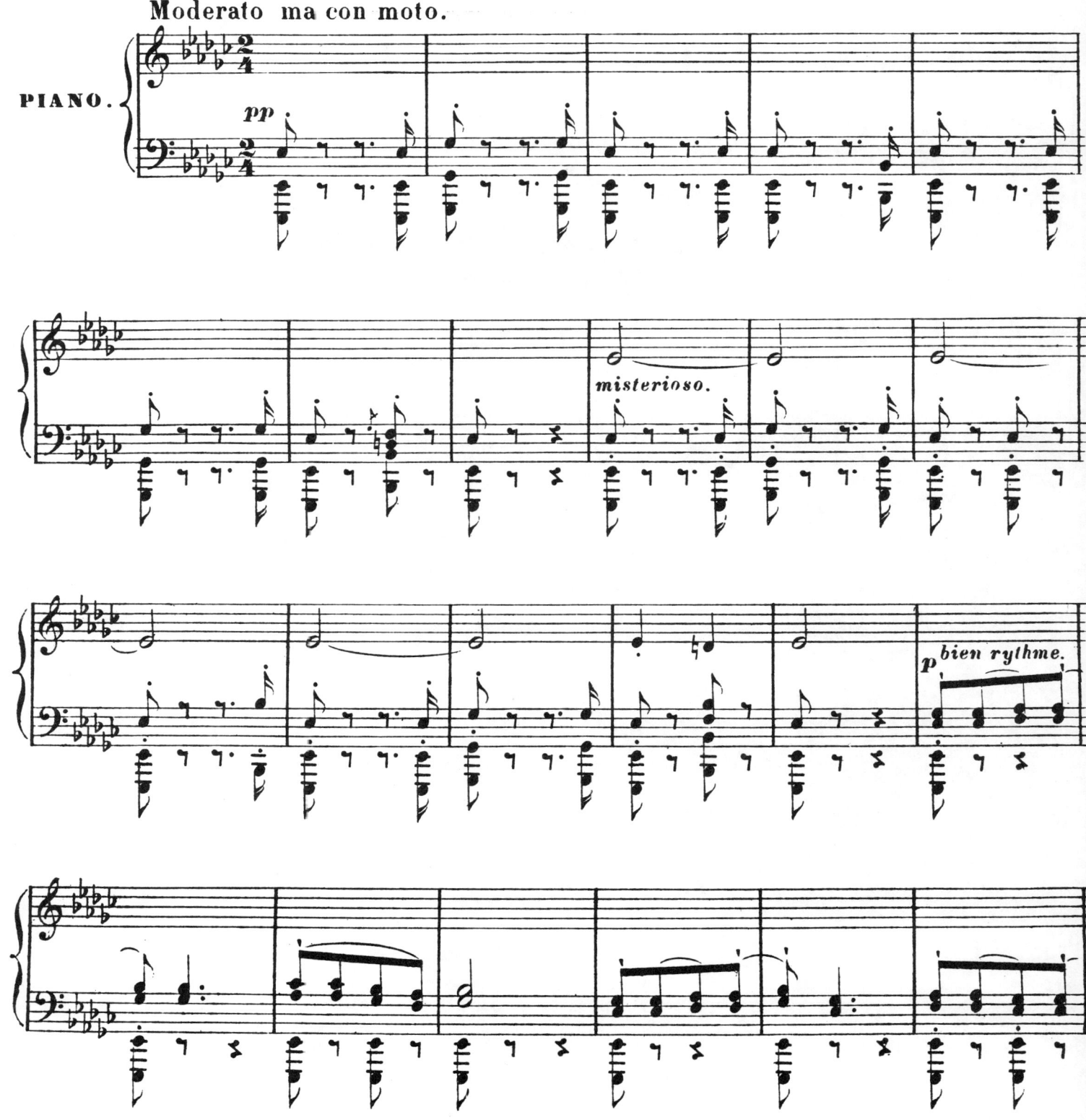

Souvenir de Porto Rico · 53

54 · Souvenir de Porto Rico

Souvenir de Porto Rico · 55

56 · Souvenir de Porto Rico

Souvenir de Porto Rico · 57

58 · Souvenir de Porto Rico

Souvenir de Porto Rico

CRYSTAL SPRING
TREMOLO.

S. A. EMERY.

Crystal Spring: Tremolo · 61

62 · Crystal Spring: Tremolo

Crystal Spring: Tremolo · 63

TO
Wm. V. Wallace.

SILVER SPRING
FOR THE
Piano Forte
by
WILLIAM MASON.

OP. 6.

10

NEW YORK
Published by Wm. A. POND & Co. 547 Broadway.

ALBANY J.H.HIDLEY. CLEVELAND S.BRAINARD & Co. CHICAGO R.G.GREENE.
ST.LOUIS W.W.WAKELAM. P.P.WERLEIN NEW ORLEANS.

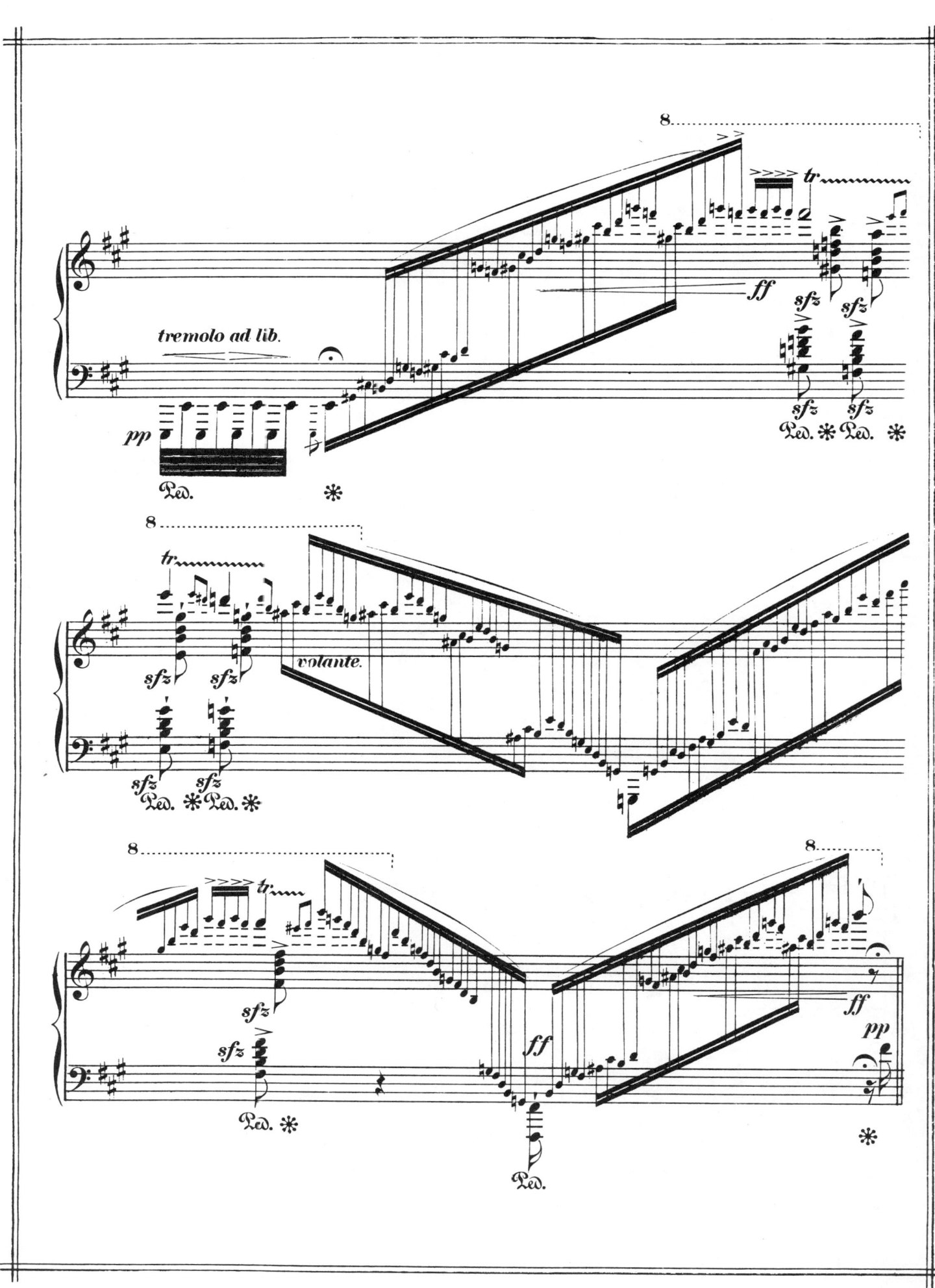

66 · Silver Spring

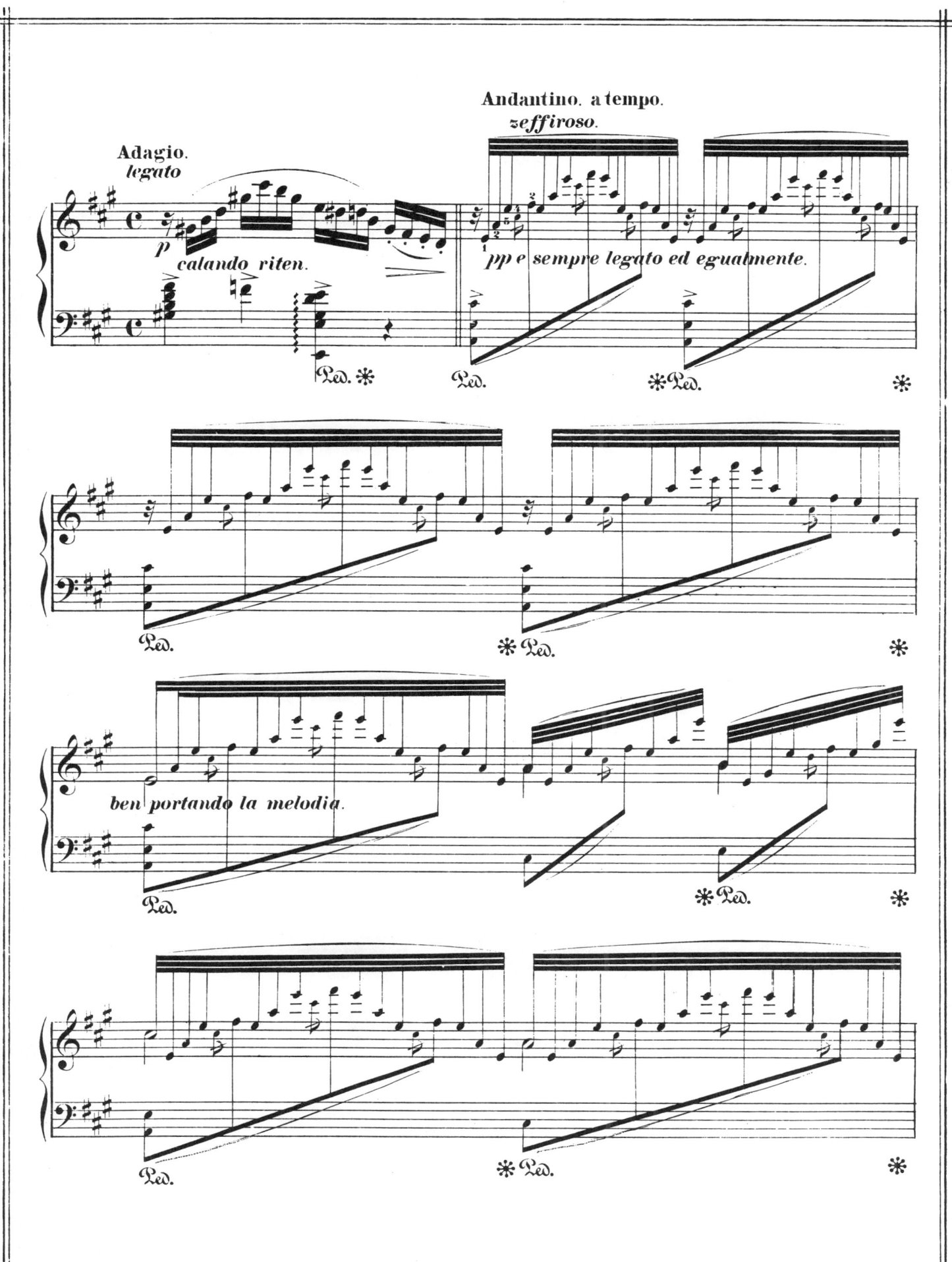

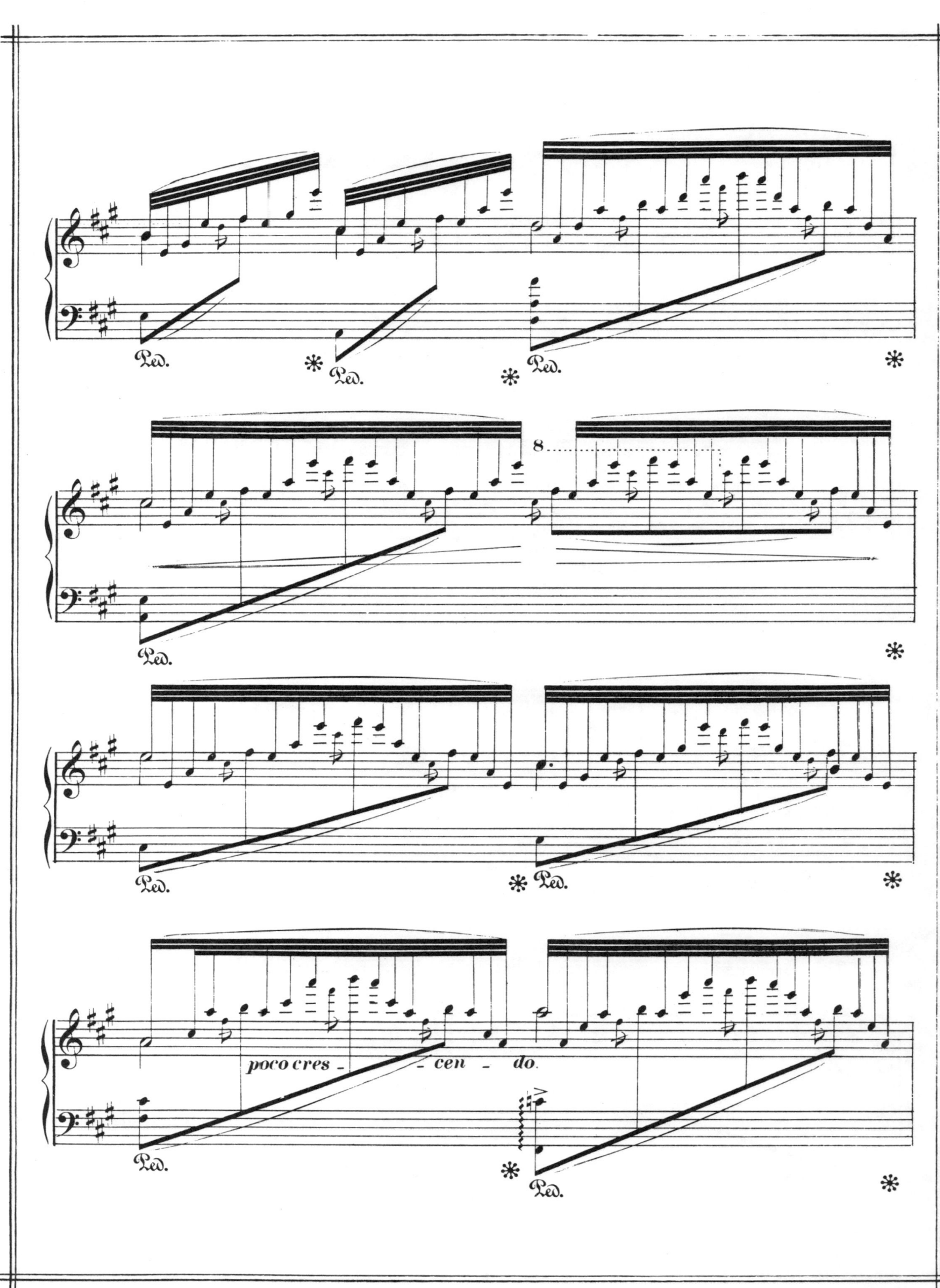

68 · Silver Spring

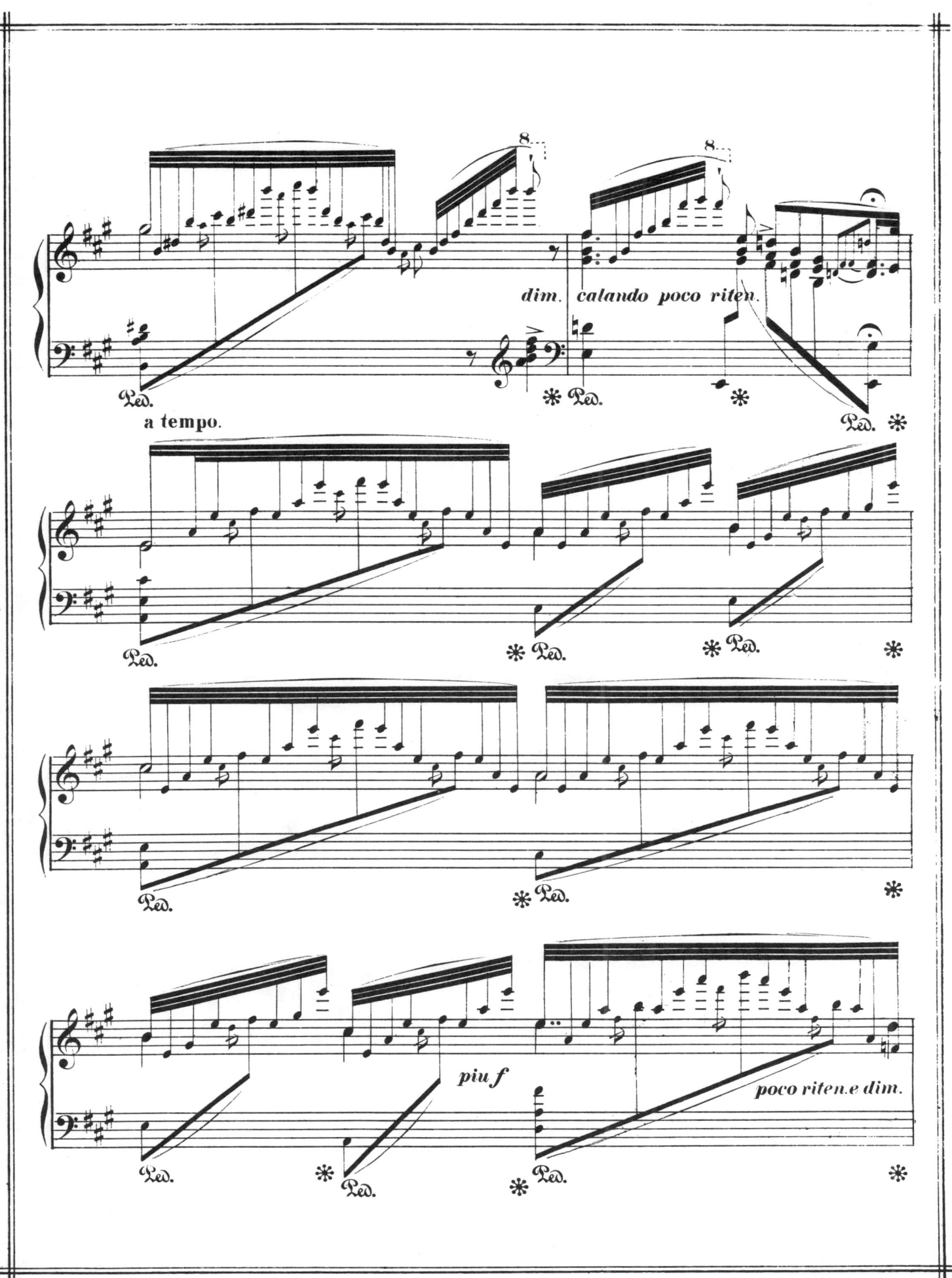

Silver Spring · 69

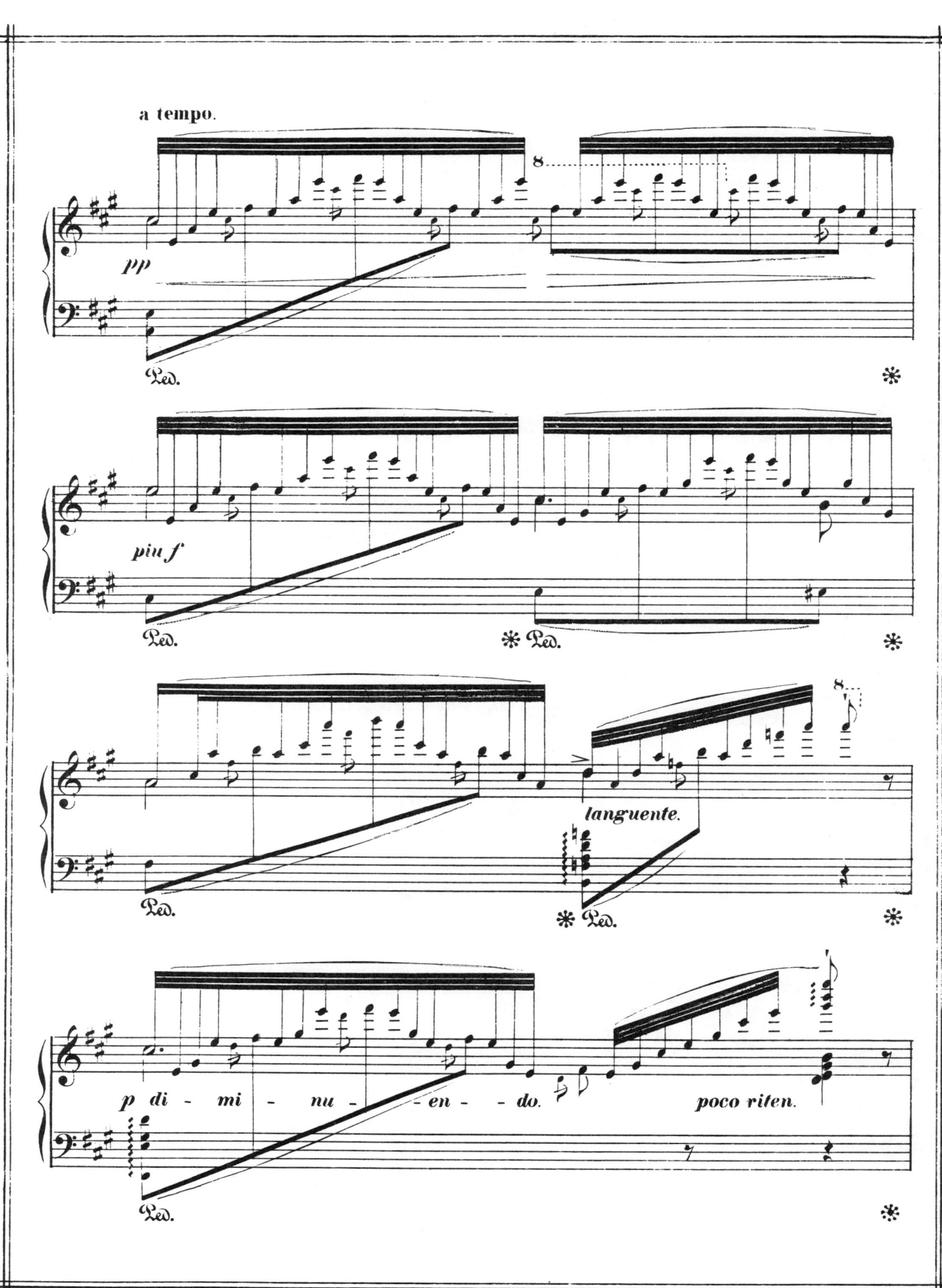

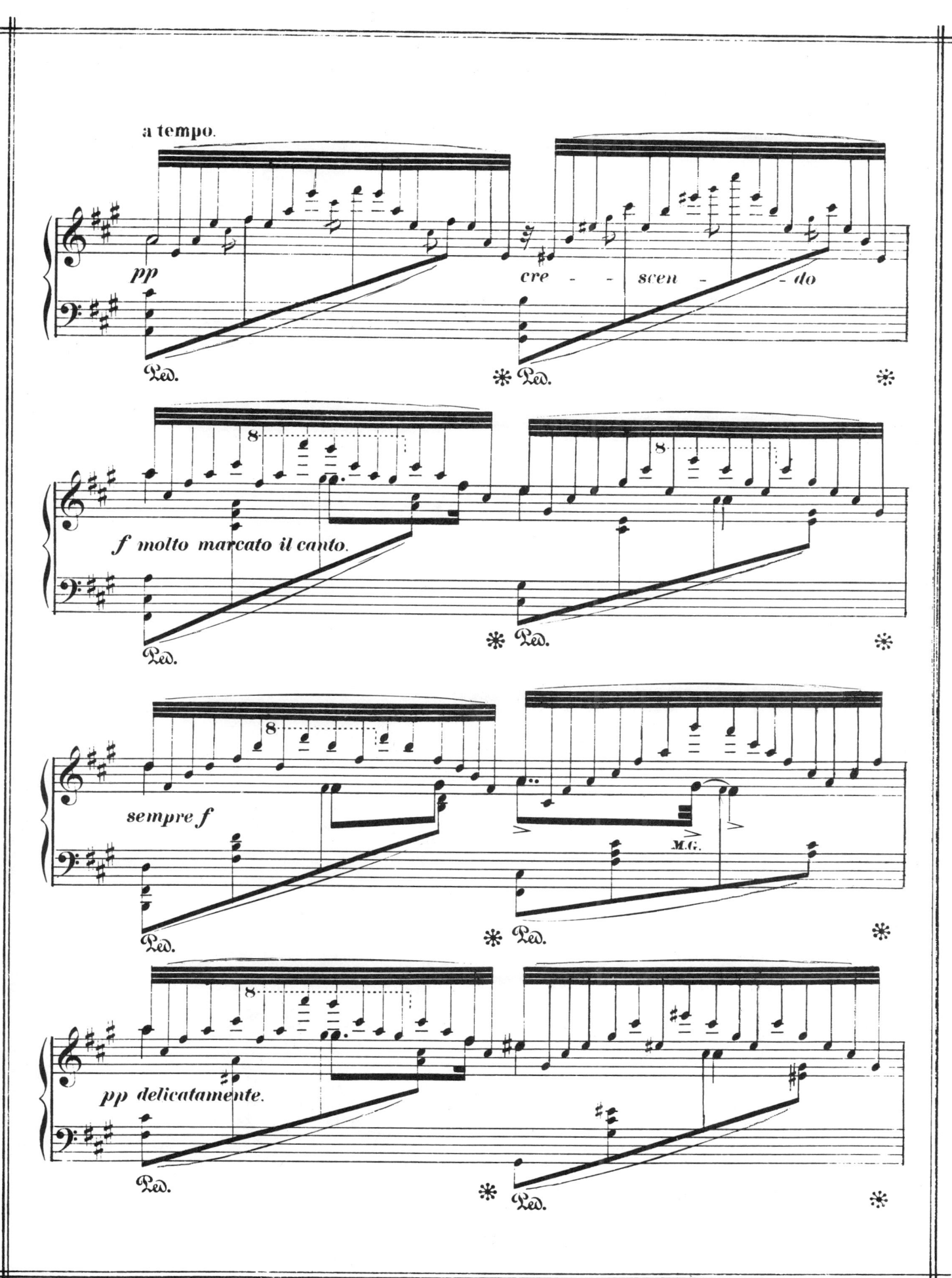

Silver Spring · 71

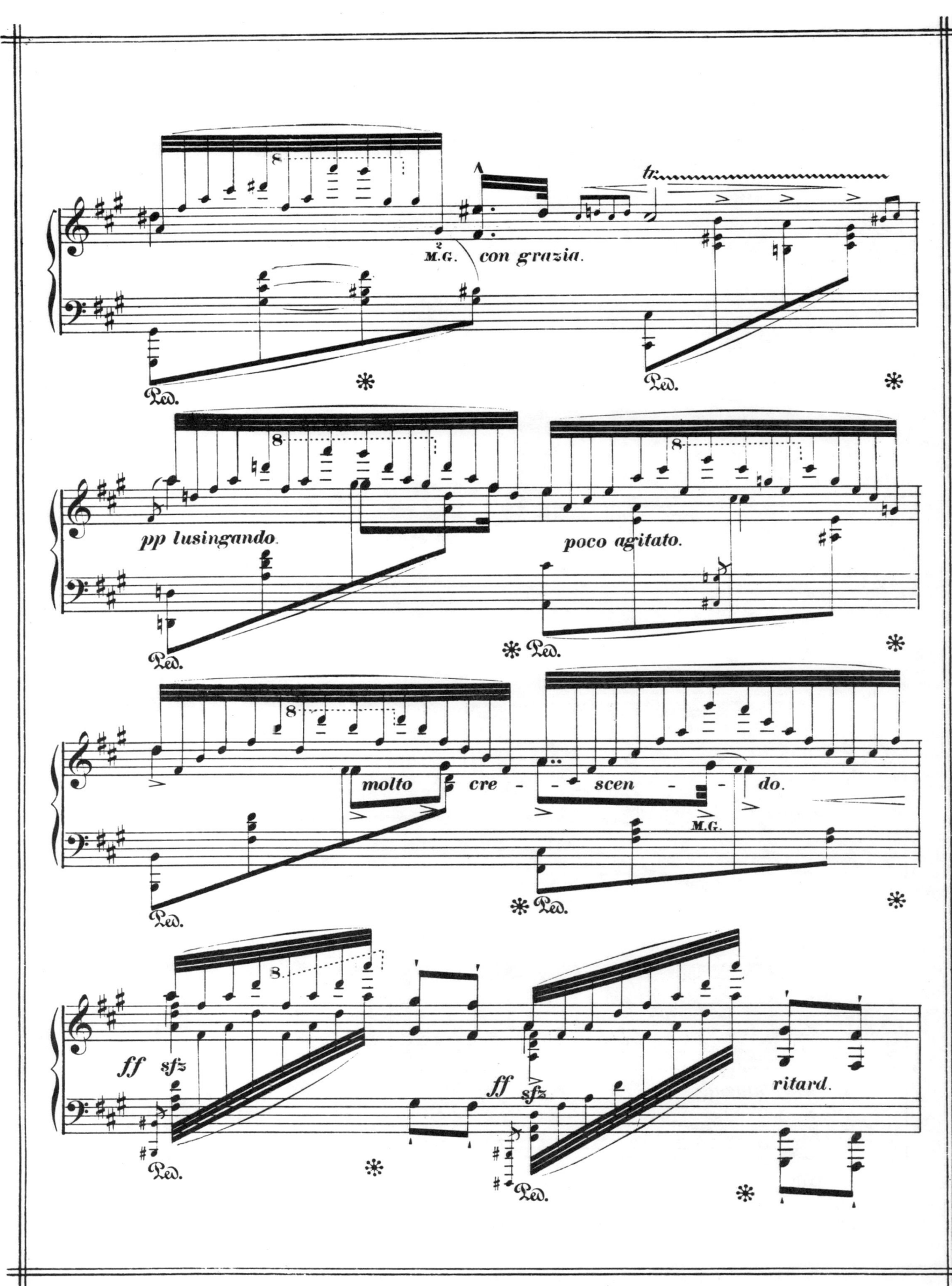

72 · Silver Spring

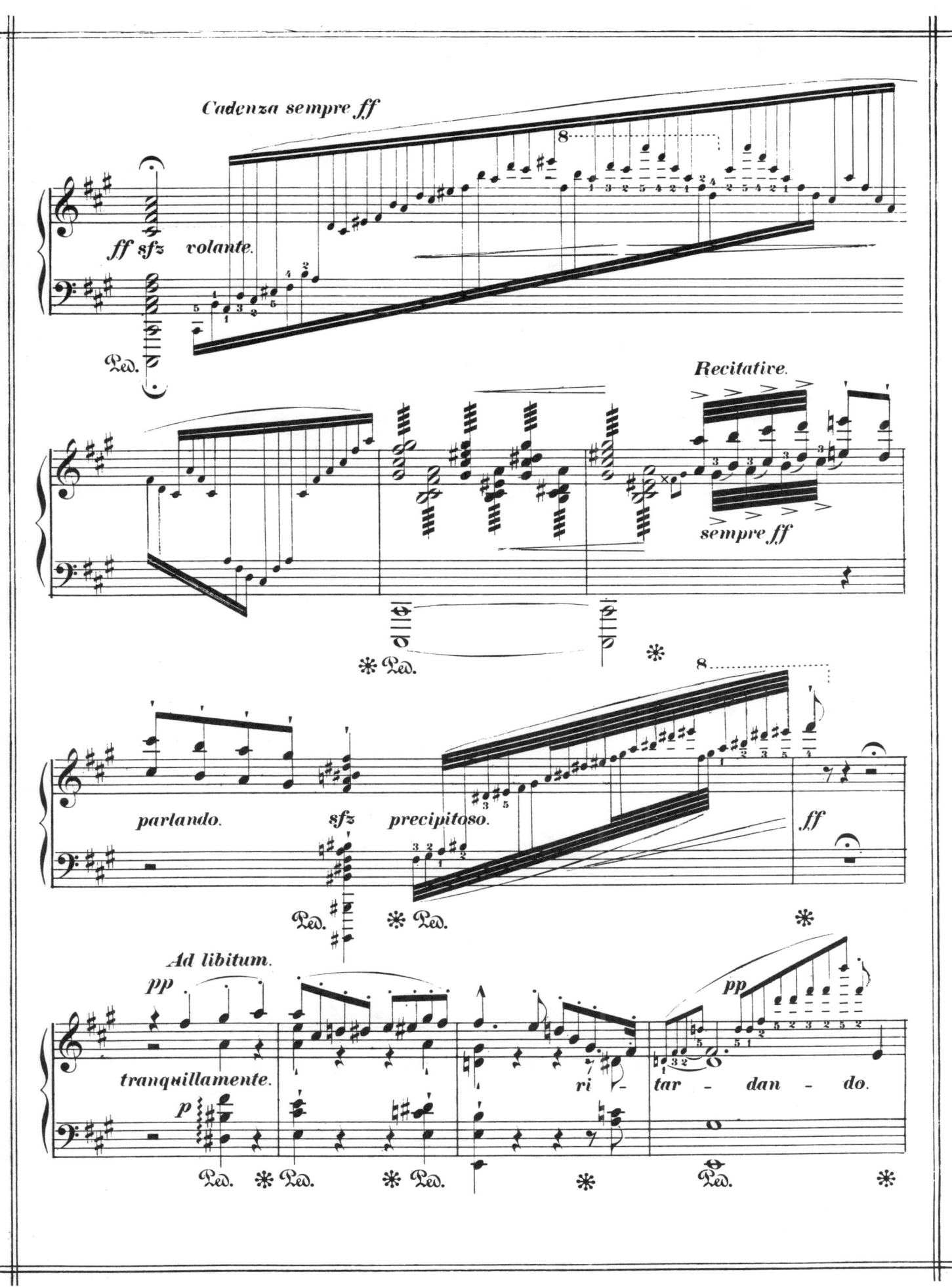

Silver Spring · 73

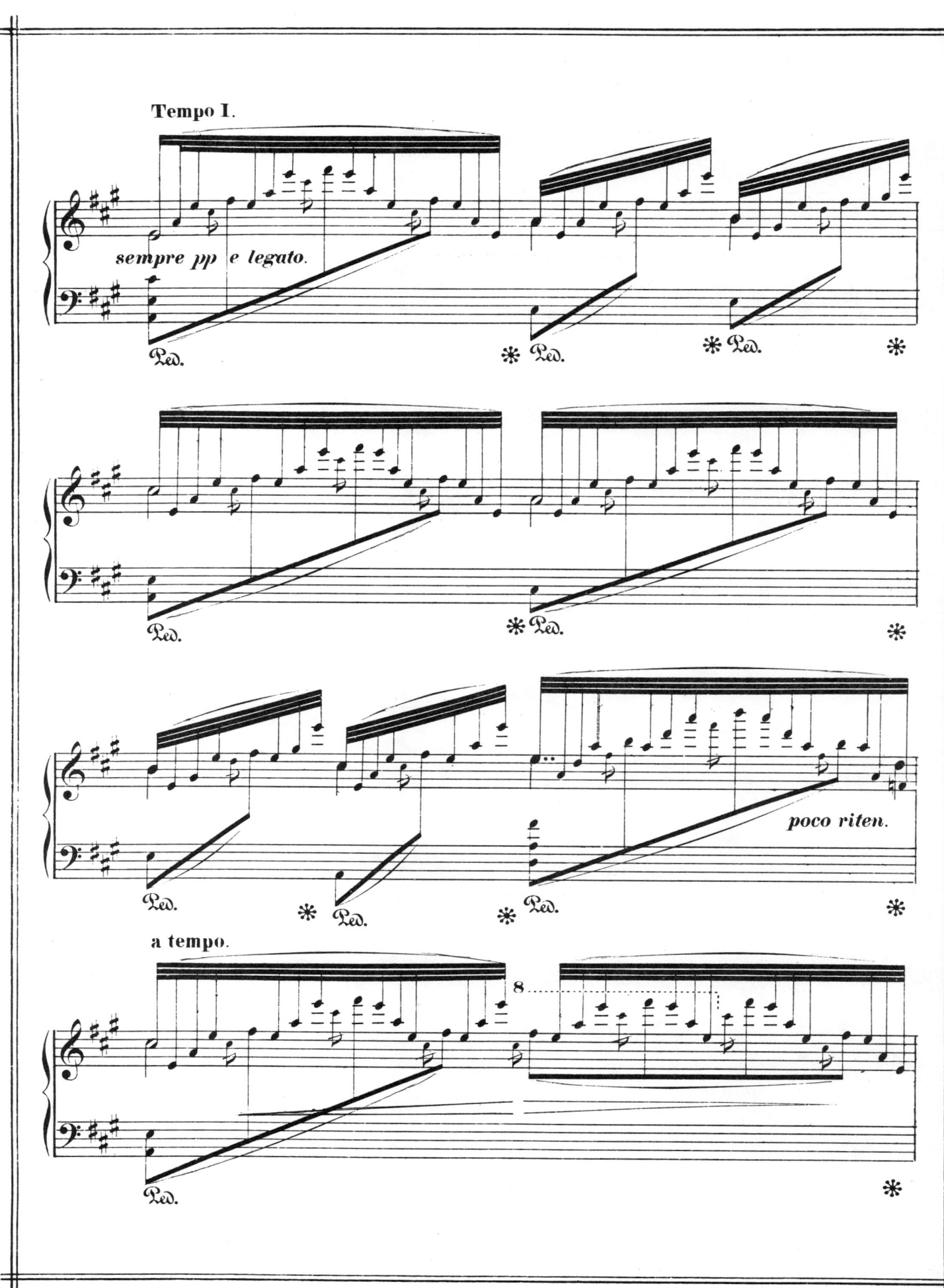

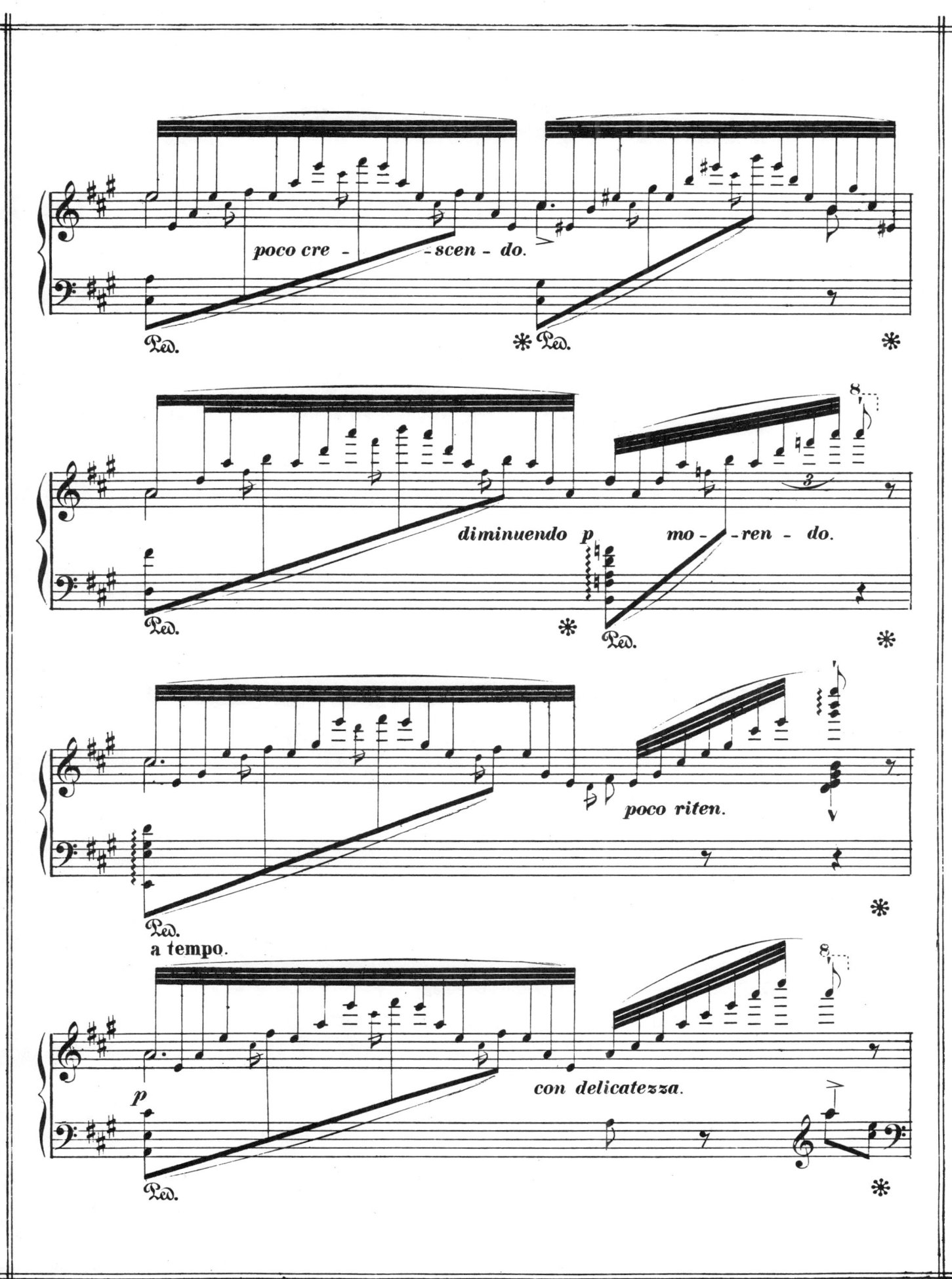

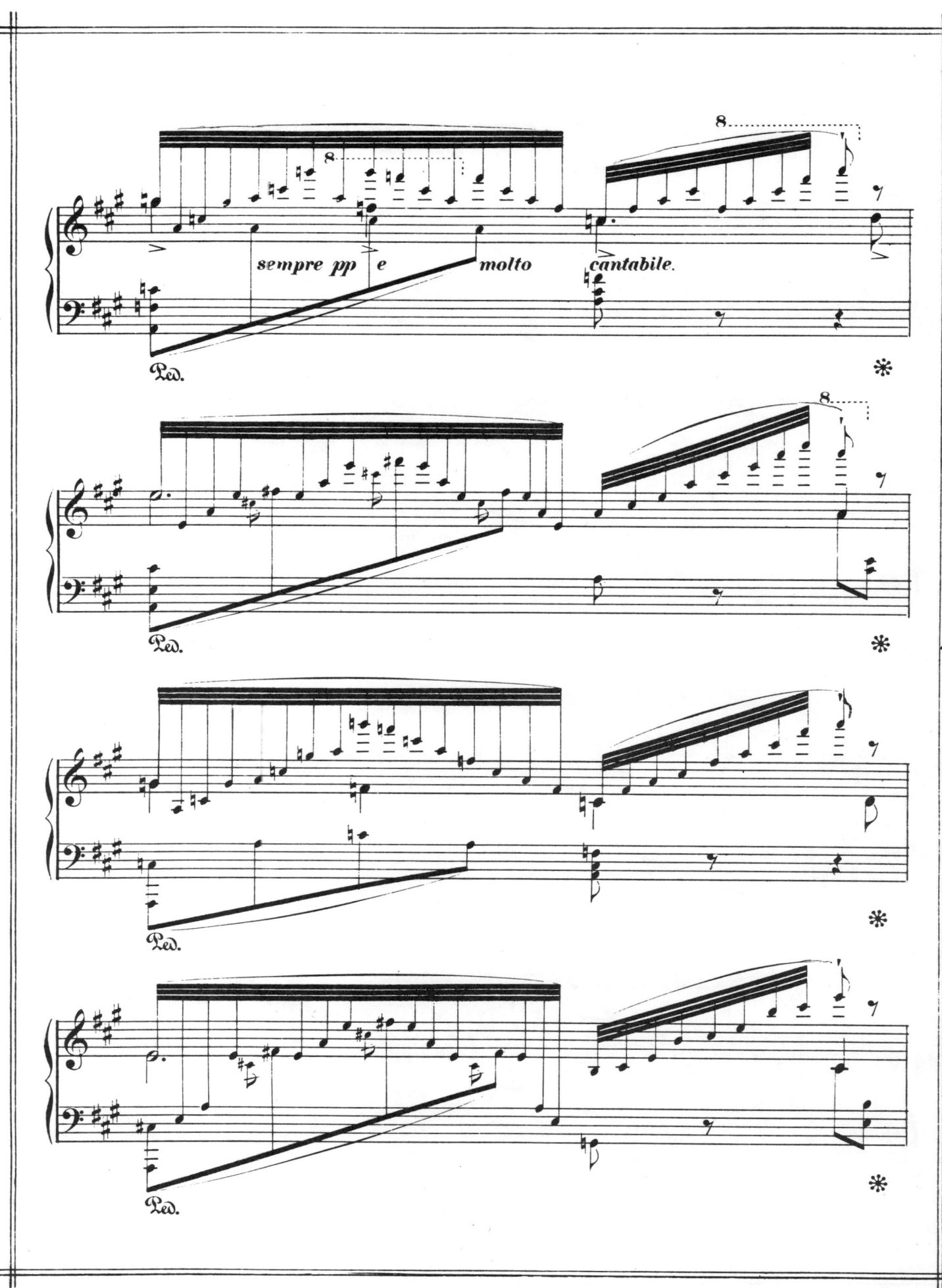

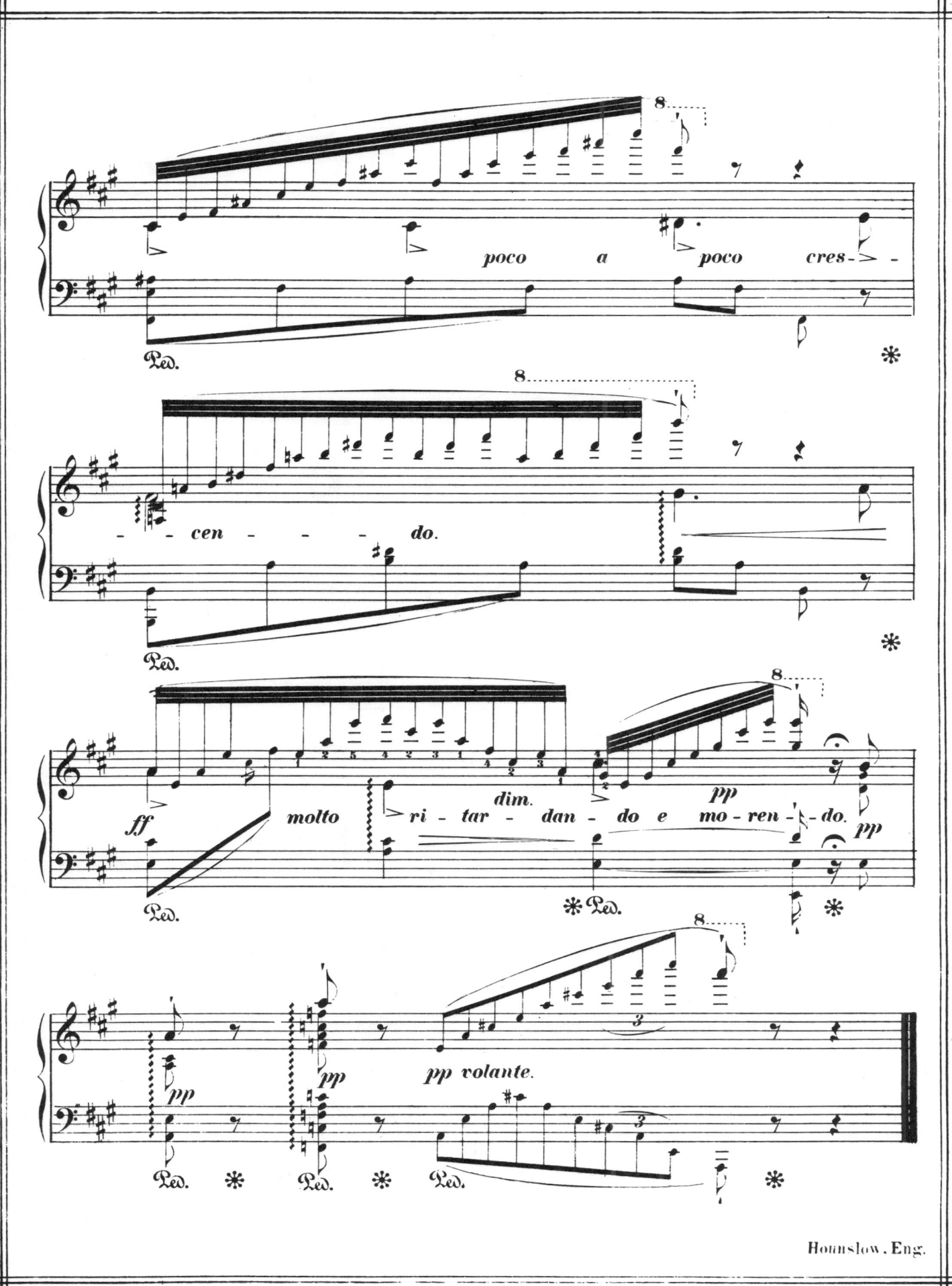

Silver Spring · 77

ANNIE & I.

SONNET. E. C. PHELPS.

80 · Annie and I

Annie and I · 83

MAPLE LEAF RAG.

BY SCOTT JOPLIN.

Tempo di marcia.

86 · Maple Leaf Rag

III. Theatrical Music

6
I drove my horss
Vay up de hill
But de oder side
Look'd rader difikil.
    Weel about &c.

7
Goin on my jerney
A lizzard boud to me
Pas on Jemes Crow
De rode is free.
    Weel about &c.

8
I jump a bord a flat boat
An vent to Nu Orlenes
An seed whar de kill'd
Ole jinrel Pakenhemes.
    Weel about &c.

9
Wen I got pon de Levey
I let my pashun luse
An John de Arms put me
In de Callyboose.
    Weel about &c.

10
I gib im a lether nine pence,
Den de let me go,
An I weel about and turn about
An jump Jim Crow.
    Weel about &c.

11
Den I cum to ole Kentukey,
Wher I hab you for to no,
Dat all de pretty ladeys Dar
Lub Jim Crow.
    Weel about &c.

12
De Ohio Niggers
Lib on mush
But the Kentukey Niggers
Say oh! hush.
    Weel about &c.

13
De Coal Black Rose
Wonce was all de go,
Till she fine a rival
In de real Jim Crow.
    Weel about &c.

14
Dars two ole Shojers
Whose names me nier forgit
One was Masse George Washington
De oder Laughayit.
    Weel about &c.

15
I neeld to de buzzard
An I bou'd to de Crow
An eb'ry time I reel'd
Why I jump't Jim Crow.
    Weel about &c.

16
You talk of Madam Ferum
An bout your Herrclime
But Herr Crow kan beat em both
An gib um 99.
    Weel about &c.

17
Wen Jim Crow is President
Of dis Unitid State
He'l drink mintjewlips
An swing pon a gate.
    Weel about &c.

18
Den go ahed wite fokes
Dont be slow,
Hop ober dubble trubble
Jump Jim Crow.
    Weel about &c.

19
So neber mine de wether,
Or how de wind do blow,
For in spite of wind an wether
Will I jump Jim Crow.
    Weel about &c.

96 · Ole Dan Tucker

2

Here's my razor in good order
Magnum bonum just a border
Sheep shell de oats ole Tucker shell de corn
And I shave you soon as my water warm.
    Get out de way &c.

3

De niggers dey come far and near
To hear him play dis ole banjo
He used to sit by de light ob de moon
And fire away dis good ole tune.
    Get out de way &c.

4

Ole Tucker lib in a little log hut
His face it was de color ob sut
His nose was flat his eye was full
And his head looked like a bag of wool.
    Get out de way &c.

5

Ole Tucker did'nt come from Guinea
But he libed in ole Virginny
He used to lib on so much fat
Dat his head so big he could'nt wear a hat.
    Get out de way &c.

6

I went up to Keeple steeple
Dare I met some colored people
Some was brack and some was bracker
Some was de color ob brown tobacco.
    Get out de way &c.

7

Way down in ole Beaver creek
De niggers grow some ten or leven feet
Dey go to bed but it aint no use
For dare feet hang out for de chicken roost.
    Get out de way &c.

8

Sheep and hog walking in de paster
Knife and fork a sticking in dare shoulder
Wonder where is ole Dan Tucker
To come and kill dis hog for supper.
    Get out de way &c.

9

Dare was a nigger in our town
He swallowed a hogshead molasses down
De molasses worked de hogshead bust
And he went up in a thunder gust.
    Get out de way &c.

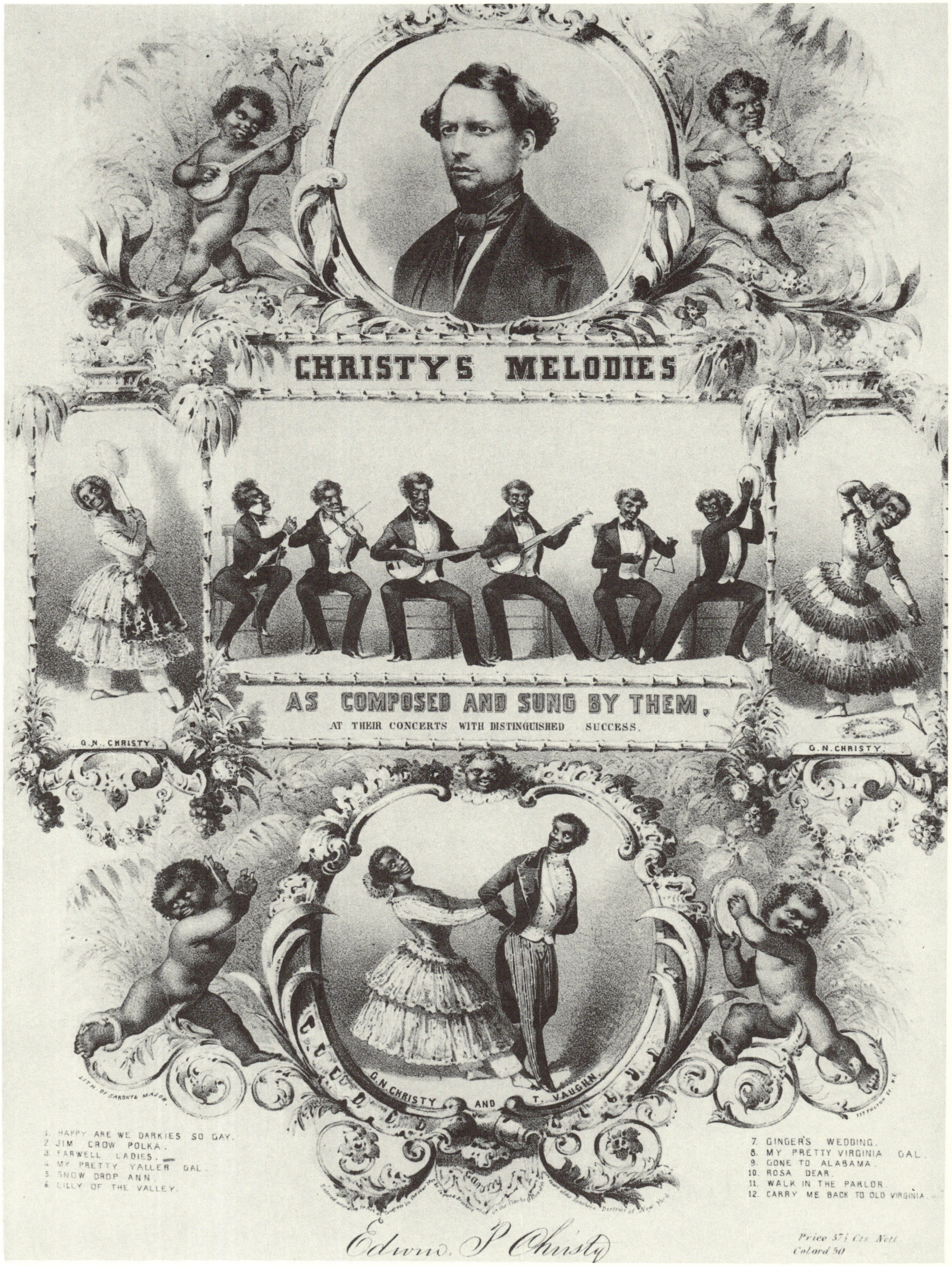

CHRISTY'S MELODIES
AS COMPOSED AND SUNG BY THEM,
AT THEIR CONCERTS WITH DISTINGUISHED SUCCESS.
G.N. CHRISTY.
G.N. CHRISTY.
G.N. CHRISTY AND T. VAUGHN.
LITH. OF SARONY & MAJOR.
1. HAPPY ARE WE DARKIES SO GAY.
2. JIM CROW POLKA.
3. FARWELL LADIES.
4. MY PRETTY YALLER GAL.
5. SNOW DROP ANN.
6. LILLY OF THE VALLEY.
7. GINGER'S WEDDING.
8. MY PRETTY VIRGINIA GAL.
9. GONE TO ALABAMA.
10. ROSA DEAR.
11. WALK IN THE PARLOR.
12. CARRY ME BACK TO OLD VIRGINIA.
Edwin. P. Christy
Price 37½ Cts Nett.
Colord 50

100 · Farewell Ladies

2

We've been all over the country through,
And seen most things, both old and new;
But of all our very great desire,
Is to have de Ladies us admire!

    Chorus. **Fare you well! Ladies &c.**

3

O, Gemb'ilmen! we thank you too,
For fatching de ladies long wid you,
To hear this darkie minstrel band,
Who sing and dance throughout the land.

    Chorus. **Fare you well! Ladies &c.**

4

Whenever again we make a call
We'll do our best to please you all:
One ting is sure, we'll neber tire,
Unless some ob us should suspire!

    Chorus. **Fare you well! Ladies &c.**

G. W. Quidor Eng'r.

2
I jumped aboard de telegrph,
And trabbelled down de riber,
De Lectric fluid magnified,
And Killed five Hundred Nigger
De bullgine buste, de horse run off,
I realy thought I'd die;
I shut my eyes to hold my breath,
Susana, dont you cry.
    Oh! Susana &c.

3
I had a dream de odder night,
When ebery ting was still;
I thought I saw Susana,
A coming down de hill.
The buckwheat cake war in her mouth,
The tear was in her eye,
Says I, im coming from de South,
Susana, dont you cry.
    Oh! Susana &c.

4
I soon will be in New Orleans,
And den I'll look all round,
And when I find Susana,
I'll fall upon the ground.
But if I do not find her,
Dis darkie 'l surely die,
And when I'm dead and buried,
Susana, dont you cry.
    Oh! Susana &c.

S. Ackerman.

NOTRE-DAME OF PARIS

A LYRICAL DRAMA IN FOUR ACTS

WORDS BY J. R. FRY MUSIC BY W. H. FRY

SOLOS AND CHORUSSES

106 · Notre-Dame of Paris: Act I, no. 8

Notre-Dame of Paris: Act I, no. 8

Notre-Dame of Paris: Act I, no. 8

112 · *Notre-Dame of Paris*: Act I, no. 8

Notre-Dame of Paris: Act I, no. 8

114 · Notre-Dame of Paris: Act I, no. 8

116 · *Notre-Dame of Paris: Act I, no. 8*

GOLDEN CHAINS.

DUETT.

From the American Opera Bouffe, EVANGELINE.

E. E. RICE.

118 · Evangeline: "Golden Chains"

Evangeline: "Golden Chains"

120 · Evangeline: "Golden Chains"

Evangeline: "Golden Chains"

122 · Evangeline: "Golden Chains"

Evangeline: "Golden Chains"

124 · Rip Van Winkle: "Who are all these folks I see?"

Rip Van Winkle: "Who are all these folks I see?"

Rip Van Winkle: "Who are all these folks I see?"

128 · Rip Van Winkle: "Who are all these folks I see?"

Rip Van Winkle: "Who are all these folks I see?"

Rip Van Winkle: "Who are all these folks I see?"

AZARA

Opera in Three Acts by

Oper in drei Akten von

John Knowles Paine

Act II, Scene 5

Azara: Act II, Scene V (vocal score) · 133

134 · *Azara:* Act II, Scene V (vocal score)

Azara: Act II, Scene V (vocal score)

136 · Azara: Act II, Scene V (vocal score)

138 · Azara: Act II, Scene V (vocal score)

Azara: Act II, Scene V (vocal score)

Azara: Act II, Scene V (vocal score)

142 · *Azara:* Act II, Scene V (vocal score)

Azara: Act II, Scene V (vocal score)

144 · *Azara:* Act II, Scene V (vocal score)

Azara: Act II, Scene V (vocal score)

146 · Azara: Act II, Scene V (vocal score)

Azara: Act II, Scene V (vocal score) · 147

148 · Azara: Act II, Scene V (vocal score)

Azara: Act II, Scene V (vocal score)

150 · Azara: Act II, Scene V (vocal score)

Azara: Act II, Scene V (vocal score) · 151

152 · *Azara:* Act II, Scene V (vocal score)

Azara: Act II, Scene V (vocal score)

154 · *Azara:* Act II, Scene V (vocal score)

IV. Choral Music

(Anthems, Glees, Hymns, Oratorios)

*BEE'SWINGS & FISH,

A Humourous Glee in Three Parts

Composed by

DIELMAN.

Baltimore, Pub.d by Geo. Willig Jun.r

*This Glee was Composed at the Fish House opposite the City of Baltimore kept by F. Reglin, while the Company were enjoying the above named *beverage.*

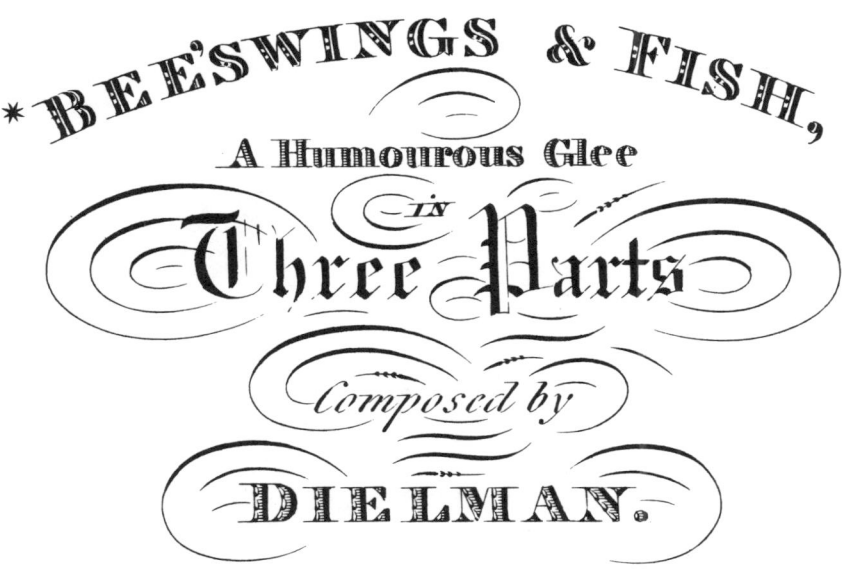

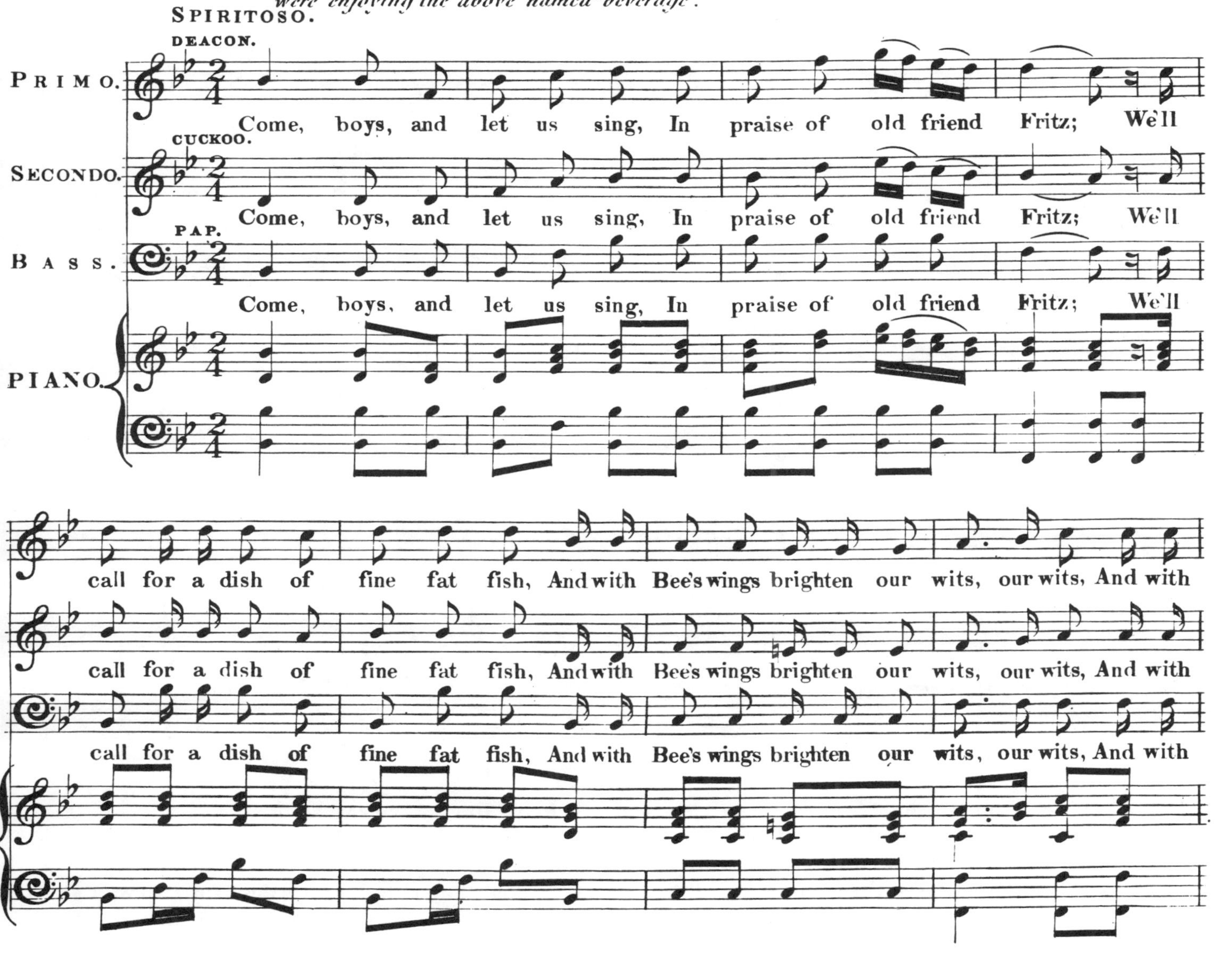

2.
Aint he a merry host?
  He has crabs— well what of that;
Let's pass out the word for a dish of hard,
  While the soft are frying in fat, in fat,
  While the soft are frying in fat.
     Bee's wings and crabs &c.

3.
Fritz sings a merry song,
  When ever he gets blue;
When hungry he feels, he traps some eels,
  And they slip down his throat in a stew, a stew,
  And they slip down his throat in a stew.
     Bee's wings and eels &c.

* In repeating the word "fish" &c. the several additions as "fried" "hard" &c. are to be applied in a humorous way.

160 · Hymn for Whitsunday

THE BOSTON HANDEL AND HAYDN SOCIETY COLLECTION OF CHURCH MUSIC;

BEING A SELECTION OF THE MOST APPROVED

PSALM AND HYMN TUNES, ANTHEMS, SENTENCES, CHANTS, &c.

TOGETHER WITH MANY BEAUTIFUL EXTRACTS FROM THE WORKS OF

HAYDN, MOZART, BEETHOVEN, AND OTHER EMINENT COMPOSERS.

HARMONIZED FOR THREE AND FOUR VOICES, WITH A FIGURED BASE FOR THE ORGAN AND PIANO FORTE

"——Assembled men, to the deep Organ join,
The long-resounding voice, oft breaking clear,
At solemn pauses, through the swelling Base;
And, as each mingling flame increases each,
In one united ardour rise to Heaven!"—*Thomson.*

EDITED BY
LOWELL MASON.

NINTH EDITION, WITH ADDITIONS AND IMPROVEMENTS.

Boston:
PUBLISHED BY RICHARDSON, LORD, AND HOLBROOK, NO. 133, WASHINGTON-STREET.
1830.

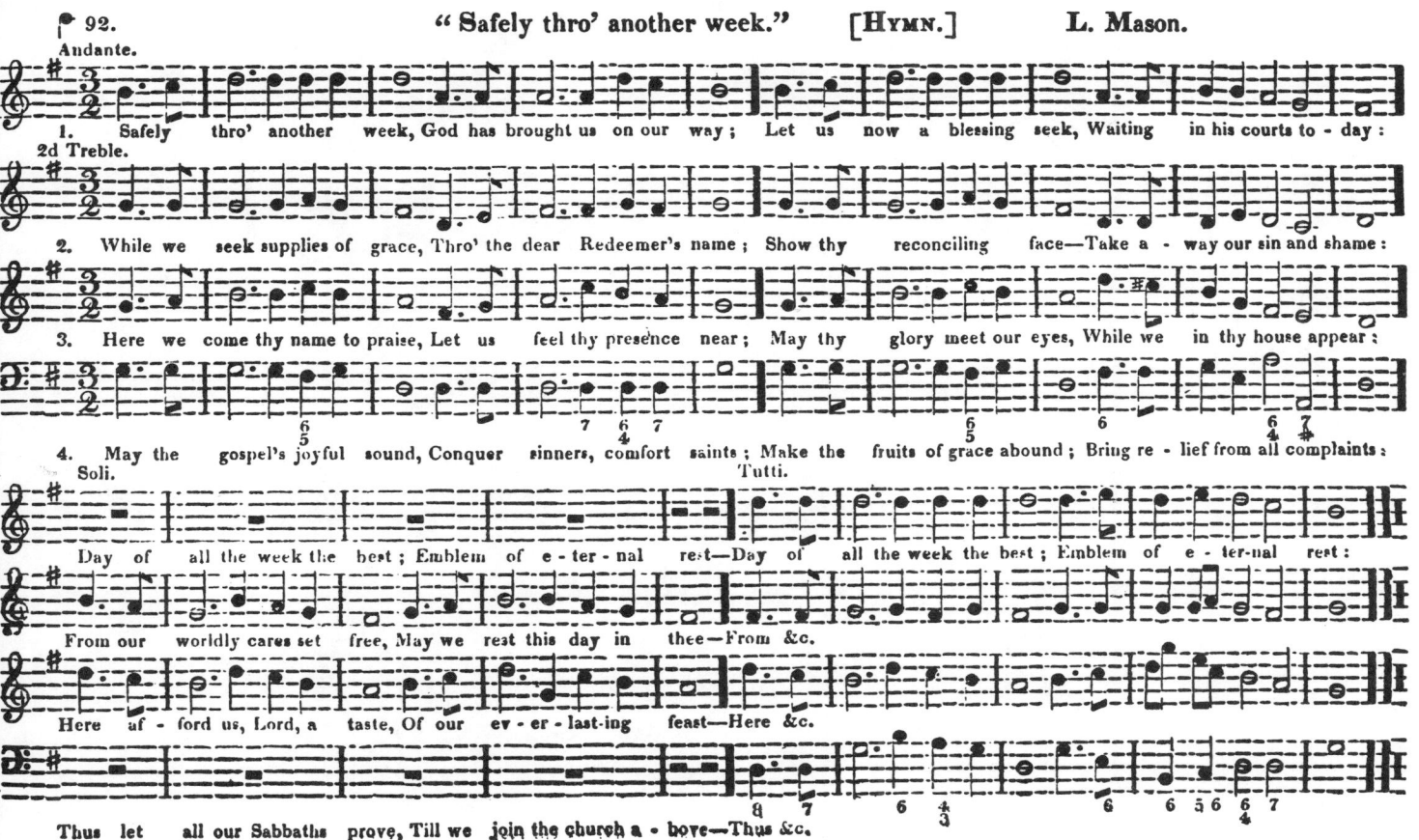

DEUX CHANSONS DES ÉLÈVES À L'ÉCOLE POLYTECHNIQUE

STUDENT SONGS

COMPOSED EXPRESSLY FOR THE ANNUAL COMMENCEMENT

OF THE

BROOKLYN COLLEGIATE & POLYTECHNIC INSTITUTE

BY

GEORGE HENRY CURTIS.

Nº 1 "Never give up" Words by M. F. Tupper.
Nº 2 "Endymion" Words by H. W. Longfellow.

NEW YORK
PUBLISHED BY FIRTH, POND & Cº 547 BROADWAY.

164 · Endymion

Endymion · 165

Praise Ye the Lord · 167

168 · Praise Ye the Lord

Praise Ye the Lord · 169

170 · Praise Ye the Lord

Praise Ye the Lord

172 · Praise Ye the Lord

Praise Ye the Lord · 173

Praise Ye the Lord · 175

176 · Praise Ye the Lord

Three Kings of Orient.

BY JOHN HENRY HOPKINS, JR.

N.B.—Each of verses 2, 3, and 4, is sung as a solo, to the music of Gaspard's part in the 1st and 5th verses, the accompaniment and chorus being the same throughout. Only verses 1 and 5 are sung as a trio. Men's voices are best for the parts of the Three Kings, but the music is set in the G clef for the accommodation of children.

GASPARD.

2. Born a KING on Bethlehem plain,
GOLD I bring to crown Him again,
King for ever,
Ceasing never
Over us all to reign.
    Chorus.—O Star, &c.

MELCHIOR.

3. FRANKINCENSE to offer have I,
Incense owns a Deity nigh:
Prayer and praising
All men raising,
Worship Him GOD on High.
    Chorus.—O Star, &c.

BALTHAZAR.

4. MYRRH is mine; its bitter perfume
Breathes a life of gathering gloom;—
Sorrowing, sighing,
Bleeding, dying,
Sealed in the stone-cold tomb.
    Chorus.—O Star, &c.

1857.

St. Peter

By JOHN KNOWLES PAINE

No. 34.   Recit. and Solo.—REPENT, AND BE BAPTISED.

Re - pent, re-pent, and be bap - tis - ed, ev' - ry one of you,

In the name of Je-sus Christ, for the forgiveness of sins, and ye shall receive the gift of the

Ho - ly Ghost.

For the prom - ise is to you and your chil - - dren, and to

all that are a - far off, as many as the Lord our God shall

RECITATIVE.—WHILE PETER YET SPAKE.

180 · St. Peter: nos. 34 and 35

No. 35. CHORUS.—THIS IS THE WITNESS OF GOD.

St. Peter: nos. 34 and 35 · 181

184 · St. Peter: nos. 34 and 35

Rock of Ages · 189

190 · Rock of Ages

Rock of Ages · 191

192 · Rock of Ages

V. Chamber Music

PENSÉES MUSICALES

À SON AMI A. DEL NERO.

pour

Piano et Violon

composées

PAR

Charles C. Perkins.

Op. 11.

Cah. II.   Deux Cahiers.   Pr: 1 Thlr: 10 Ngr.

Propriété des Editeurs.

Leipzig, chez Breitkopf & Härtel.

Enregistré aux Archives de l'Union.

Eind Sta Gall.

9050 & 51.

Pensées musicales: "Bolero"

198 · Pensées musicales: "Bolero"

Pensées musicales: "Bolero"

200 · Pensées musicales: "Bolero"

Pensées musicales: "Bolero" · 201

Allegro de Concert
(Quartette for Saxophones)

Caryl Florio
(1879)

Allegro de Concert · 203

204 · Allegro de Concert

Allegro de Concert · 205

206 · Allegro de Concert

Allegro de Concert · 207

208 · Allegro de Concert

210 · Allegro de Concert

Allegro de Concert · 211

212 · *Allegro de Concert*

Allegro de Concert · 213

214 · Allegro de Concert

Allegro de Concert · 215

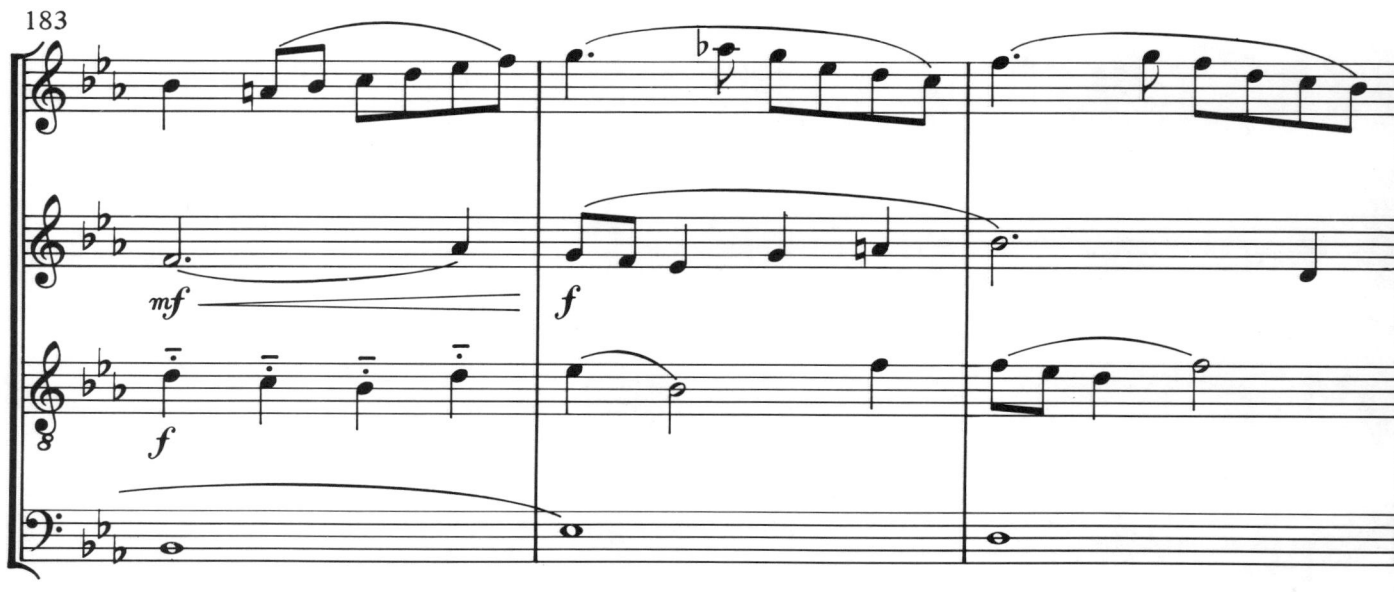

216 · *Allegro de Concert*

Allegro de Concert · 217

218 · Allegro de Concert

Allegro de Concert · 219

220 · *Allegro de Concert*

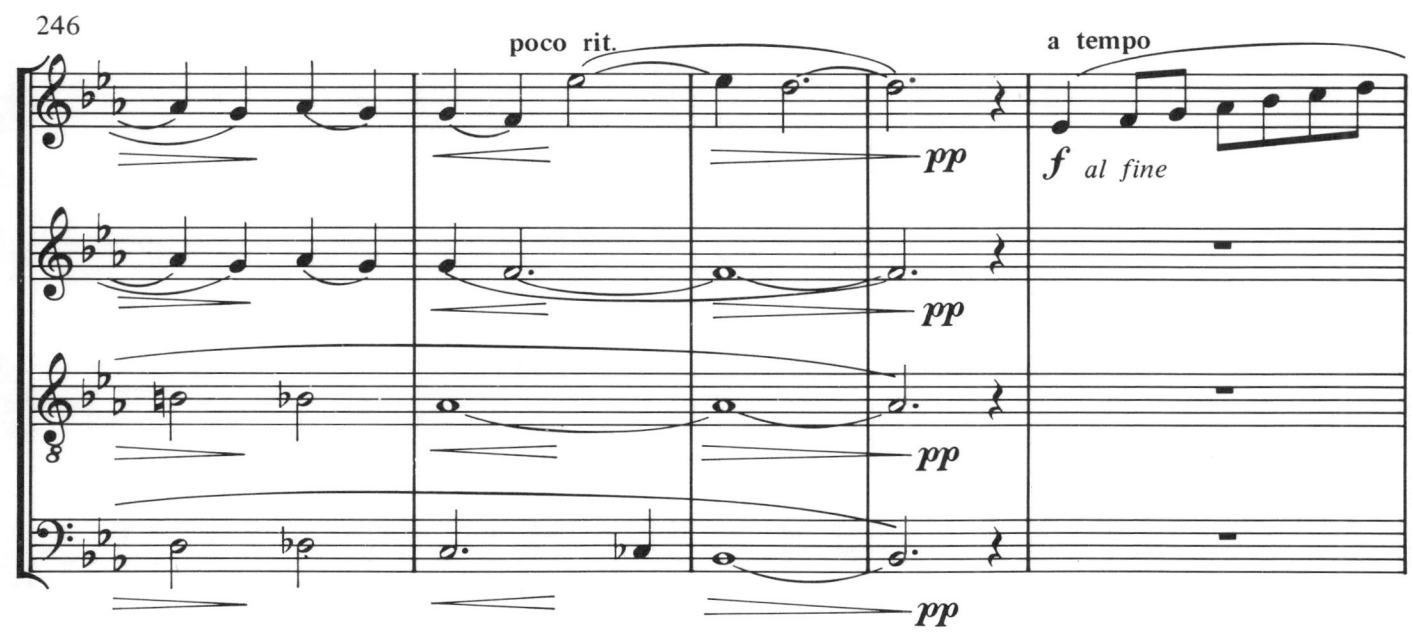

Allegro de Concert · 221

222 · Allegro de Concert

*The following 12 measures appear only in the manuscript parts, where they are on strips pasted loosely over the concluding measures of the *Andante*. The passage was presumably used in performance as a brief alternate or additional introduction to the *Allegro* fugal section.

This work is available separately from the publisher as a performing edition with score and parts.

224 · Allegro de Concert

VI. Orchestra Music

228 · Beach's *Piano Concerto:* last movement

230 · Beach's *Piano Concerto:* last movement

Beach's *Piano Concerto:* last movement

232 · Beach's *Piano Concerto:* last movement

Beach's *Piano Concerto:* last movement · 233

234 · Beach's *Piano Concerto:* last movement

Beach's *Piano Concerto*: last movement · 235

236 · Beach's *Piano Concerto:* last movement

Beach's *Piano Concerto*: last movement

238 · Beach's *Piano Concerto:* last movement

Beach's *Piano Concerto:* last movement

240 · Beach's *Piano Concerto:* last movement

Beach's *Piano Concerto:* last movement · 241

242 · Beach's *Piano Concerto:* last movement

Beach's *Piano Concerto:* last movement

244 · Beach's *Piano Concerto:* last movement

Beach's *Piano Concerto:* last movement

246 · Beach's *Piano Concerto:* last movement

Beach's *Piano Concerto:* last movement · 247

248 · Beach's *Piano Concerto:* last movement

Beach's *Piano Concerto*: last movement · 249

250 · Beach's *Piano Concerto:* last movement

Beach's *Piano Concerto:* last movement · 251

(Symphonic Sketches: I)
Jubilee

G. W. CHADWICK

Jubilee (Symphonic Sketches: I) · 253

254 · Jubilee (Symphonic Sketches: I)

Jubilee (Symphonic Sketches: I) · 255

256 · Jubilee (Symphonic Sketches: I)

Jubilee (Symphonic Sketches: I) · 257

258 · Jubilee (Symphonic Sketches: I)

Jubilee (Symphonic Sketches: I) · 259

260 · Jubilee (Symphonic Sketches: I)

Jubilee (Symphonic Sketches: I) · 261

262 · Jubilee (Symphonic Sketches: I)

Jubilee (Symphonic Sketches: I) · 263

264 · Jubilee (Symphonic Sketches: I)

Jubilee (Symphonic Sketches: I) · 265

266 · Jubilee (Symphonic Sketches: I)

Jubilee (Symphonic Sketches: I) · 267

268 · Jubilee (Symphonic Sketches: I)

Jubilee (Symphonic Sketches: I) · 269

270 · Jubilee (Symphonic Sketches: I)

Jubilee (Symphonic Sketches: I) · 271

272 · Jubilee (Symphonic Sketches: I)

Jubilee (Symphonic Sketches: I) · 273

274 · Jubilee (Symphonic Sketches: I)

Jubilee (Symphonic Sketches: I) · 275

276 · Jubilee (Symphonic Sketches: I)

Jubilee (Symphonic Sketches: I) · 277

278 · Jubilee (Symphonic Sketches: I)

Jubilee (Symphonic Sketches: I) · 279

280 · Jubilee (Symphonic Sketches: I)

282 · Jubilee (Symphonic Sketches: I)

Jubilee (Symphonic Sketches: I) · 283

284 · Jubilee (Symphonic Sketches: I)

Jubilee (Symphonic Sketches: I) · 285

286 · Jubilee (Symphonic Sketches: I)

288 · Jubilee (Symphonic Sketches: I)

Jubilee (Symphonic Sketches: I) · 289

290 · Jubilee (Symphonic Sketches: I)

Biographical Sketches

ASAHEL ABBOT(T) was born in 1805 in a New Hampshire village and died on Nov. 10, 1889 in Brooklyn, N.Y. He is mainly known to music scholarship through one mention in John Tasker Howard's book *Our American Music* (4th ed., 1965, p. 249). There are also notices and reviews of at least one New York performance of his oratorio *The Waldenses*. There are a few published musical pieces by Abbott, such as the song reprinted here, and at least one prose piece (there were perhaps others): the 1849 pamphlet *Eternal Punishment according to the Scriptures*.

Other than the above, easily available material by and about Abbott is very scarce. If one can trust an anonymous article about him in New York's *Sun* of Sun., Mar. 16, 1890, p. 19, he had a rather strange life. To quote the article directly:

> His health broke down while he was yet in his teens, and he went off into the logging camps to recover. From there he started to walk to Andover, Mass., where he had spent a term in the grammar school. Snows were deep and walking was not easy. He gave it up when he had got as far as Dartmouth, N.H., and taught school for awhile.... He wrote pamphlets against everything and everybody that displeased him, and even tackled ... the principal of the school.

The article tells us that Abbott knew and practiced music all this time and that upon completion of his first oratorio (there were eleven—fully orchestrated—according to the article), Abbott sent it to LOWELL MASON* for an opinion. Mason "declared that it was too classical for Americans; that the composer would better write simpler matter or go to Germany, where such work would be appreciated." After this, the article says, Abbott went to work in a saw mill.

"When he was 22 [in 1827?] Mr. Abbott left the New England saw mill and came to New York," states the article. But "he met with uniform rejections" by the publishers, and there apparently followed a vagabond period of over thirty years when Abbott lived in small New Jersey and New York towns, in Philadelphia, in Charleston, S.C., and in New York before settling in Brooklyn in 1863.

In the Feb. 1, 1850 issue of the New York periodical the *Message Bird*, a notice appeared advertising Abbott as "Prof. Music" at 144 Hammond Street (later West 11th Street). There was also an informative announcement near this notice which read: "Asahel Abbott (editor of the American Minstrel and other musical works, and long known as a successful teacher of musical composition in all its branches), respectfully gives notice that he continues to give lessons in composition, singing, and also on the piano-forte and organ.... Mr. A refers to Geo. H. Curtis, G.T. [sic] Root and others of his former pupils" (vol. 1, no. 13, p. 223). *The American Minstrel* referred to above is a book of songs and hymns published in New York by the firm of C.M. Saxton in 1849. It was co-edited by Abbott and George Andrews, contains many original Abbott compositions, and some by CURTIS (2) and DEEMS (1) among others.

The *Sun* article tells us that while Abbott did make his living in Brooklyn as a piano teacher, he refused to promote his musical compositions. He was apparently little known to his contemporaries as a composer, though GEORGE WILLIAM WARREN, among other organists, did perform Abbott's *Aria Fugata* from manuscript.

The *Sun* article gives initial publication to three of Abbott's pieces and a portion of a fourth, refers to a "manuscript autobiography," and reports that among "volumes and volumes of [music] manuscripts" that were "stacked in his house at 833 Dean Street, Brooklyn, where his wife and son still live," were, besides the eleven oratorios, "an uncounted number of piano pieces, contrapuntal compositions for the organ, anthems, secular choruses, hymns and songs." (One wonders what happened to all of these pieces. Recent efforts by this writer to learn their whereabouts have failed.)

The works of Abbott we are concerned with here date from the 1850s. The song reprinted here was published in 1850. The 1852 performance of his apparently unpublished oratorio *The Waldenses* was held in New York's Tabernacle and was conducted by GEORGE FREDERICK BRISTOW, with vocal soloists, with the New York Sacred

---

*Capital and small capital letters are used for a first reference in each sketch to composers whose biographical sketch also appears in this Anthology.

Harmonic Society (to which Abbott was one of thirty-six "councillors"), and with accompaniment played by GEORGE HENRY CURTIS (*The Musical World and Journal of the Fine Arts*, vol. 3, no. 20, p. 336).

We learn from an anonymous review in the *Musical World and Journal of the Fine Arts* that all of the oratorio, however, was not performed: the concert, "owing to frequent *encores*, was protracted to a late hour, and it was found necessary to omit a few pieces near the close" (vol. 3, no. 21, p. 357). The same review contains the following not exactly flattering remarks: "The design of the Oratorio is peculiar. It is made principally of solos and quartets, with several short and a few long choruses, none of which is of any great difficulty. As an Oratorio, it belongs to the second rank . . ." (vol. 3, no. 21, p. 357).

The review also comments on the use of keyboard rather than orchestra accompaniment (which use, it says, was "in accordance with the author's wish"): "while without an orchestra there was less of dramatic effect, there was, in its stead, a graver, serener influence, which accorded well with the religious character of the work . . . if we would have Oratorios of this class got up beyond the limits of our great cities, all the accompaniment needed would be a piano or organ" (vol. 3, no. 21, p. 357).

The *Musical Times* praised the performers (identifying Curtis as playing the organ), liked in the work "an absence of any attempt at display or clap trap," but found "a far too ponderous and grave quality of music altogether" (vol. 5, no. 7, p. 74).

The book *Choice Pearls; or, Gems of Literature* (New York: A.B. Burdick, [n.d.]), for which Abbott supplied five music compositions and one arrangement, contains a two-page, four-voice excerpt from *The Waldenses* entitled "Hymn to Solitude."

The *Sun* article about Abbott reported that a friend once asked him "if he hoped to gain recognition for his compositions. He replied: 'Perhaps after I am dead people will take them up and decide that they were worth doing.'"

BIBLIOGRAPHY

Brooklyn Eagle, Mon., Nov. 11, 1889, p. 5 [Abbott's death notice].

Dwight's Journal of Music 1:12 (Sat., June 26, 1852), 95.

The Message Bird 1:5 (Oct. 1, 1849), 76–77, [81]; 1:6 (Oct. 15, 1849), 93–94; 1:7 (Nov. 1, 1849), 116; 1:9 (Dec. 1, 1849), 140–41, 146.

The Musical World and Journal of the Fine Arts 3:14 (Mar. 14, 1852), 199.

AMY MARCY CHENEY BEACH was born on Sept. 5, 1867 in Henniker, N.H. and died on Dec. 27, 1944 in New York. She was a child prodigy in both piano and composition and was one of three women composers who could be said to belong to the so-called Second New England School (the other women were Clara Kathleen Rogers and Margaret Ruthven Lang; the male members are usually said to be JOHN KNOWLES PAINE, Horatio Parker, GEORGE W. CHADWICK, Arthur Foote, and EDWARD MACDOWELL). On Dec. 2, 1885 she was married to the physician Henry Harris Aubrey Beach, remaining his wife until Dr. Beach died in 1910. Beginning at the time of her marriage, she was known professionally as Mrs. H. H. A. Beach.

She later wrote in a letter to John Tasker Howard (May 2, 1930): "It seems as if a century must separate my earlier life, (devoted mostly to composition in my own home with occasional concert appearances), and that of recent years . . ." (a copy of this letter is in The New York Public Library, Music Division, classmark: *MNY-Amer.). Her husband was reportedly most understanding of his talented young wife, yet (as she later told an

Amy Marcy Cheney Beach
(Mrs. H. H. A. Beach)
Photograph, date unknown, as used in
Louis Elson's *Woman's Work in Music*
(1903)

interviewer) she "did all the duties of a doctor's wife.... Don't ask me how I did it! I don't know" (unsourced, undated newspaper article in the Crawford scrapbook).

Mrs. Beach composed a symphony (the *Gaelic*, op. 32, 1896)—certainly the first *well-known* symphony by an American woman; Constance Fauntleroy Runcie may have composed a symphony earlier—, a quintet for piano and strings (1908) and thirteen other chamber works, piano pieces, a mass (1891) and numerous other choral works, an opera (*Cabildo*, 1932), and about one hundred and fifty songs.

Mrs. Beach performed her *Piano Concerto in C-sharp Minor*, op. 45, composed in 1899, with the Boston Symphony Orchestra (première, Apr. 6, 1900; conductor, Wilhelm Gericke) and with other orchestras in the United States and in Europe. It is dedicated to the Venezuelan pianist Teresa Carreño (1853–1917). After the première, the *Boston Saturday Evening Gazette* in its issue of Apr. 8, 1900 mentioned that "the most brilliant portion of the work ... is the last movement" (quoted in *Mrs. H. H. A. Beach*, p. 121). Among other comments about the work, the Boston *Daily Advertiser* said on Apr. 9, 1900 that "the *finale* seemed to us the best, most decisive and most original movement of the work. The entire movement was interesting and had many bold and striking contrasts. The public ... recalled the composer-pianist four times and also added floral tributes" (quoted in *Mrs. H. H. A. Beach*, p. 122). After a St. Louis performance of the concerto, Richard L. Stokes wrote in the *St. Louis Post Dispatch* that "in these days of motor cars and telephone, her inspiration does not saunter along on foot, but travels with the velocity of a Twentieth Century express" (undated review in the Crawford scrapbook).

The two-piano version, of which the last movement is reprinted here, was published in Boston (c1900) by the Arthur P. Schmidt Company, Mrs. Beach's chief publisher for years, as it was that of many other American composers of her generation. As was typical with other "classical" American music works of the time, the language of the title page was German, and so the key of the concerto became Cis-moll.

"From 1911 until 1914 I travelled in Europe," Mrs. Beach once told an interviewer, "and gave concerts there.... My husband and my mother died almost at the same time and since then I have been a vagabond. I have no permanent home..." (unsourced, undated newspaper interview conducted by Eileen McCann found in the Crawford scrapbook). But she eventually (ca. 1916) settled in New York.

The concerto has been recorded by pianist Mary Louise Boehm-Kooper with orchestra on the Turnabout label (no. 34665-Q).

BIBLIOGRAPHY

Block, Adrienne Fried. Letter postmarked Aug. 21, 1984 to this author.

Crawford, Rebekah. *Scrapbook of clippings, photographs, programs, etc. relating to Mrs. H. H. A. Beach*. Given to the Music Division of the Library of Congress by Mrs. Crawford, Feb. 1931. (LC card number: ML410.B36 C7 case).

Mrs. H. H. A. Beach. Boston: Arthur P. Schmidt, 1906.

Tick, Judith. "Amy Marcy Cheney Beach." *The New Grove Dictionary of Music and Musicians* II, 318. London: Macmillan Publishers, 1980.

GEORGE FREDERICK BRISTOW, who was born in Brooklyn, N.Y. on Dec. 19, 1825 and died in Manhattan on Dec. 13, 1898, was the son of the English immigrant William Richard Bristow (1803–1867), organist at New York's St. Patrick's Cathedral (then at Prince and Mott streets) and solo clarinetist in the orchestra of New York's Euterpean Society. George Frederick Bristow received organ and piano lessons and was an accomplished violinist and conductor. For thirty-six years (1843–79) he was a member of the first-violin section of the New York Philharmonic, which he joined when he was seventeen. One reads on page 27 of the *Musical Courier* for Dec. 1, 1898 that Bristow "was a bitter opponent of everything foreign ... Mr. Krehbiel quotes him as once saying: 'The Philharmonic Society has been as anti-American as if it had been located in London during the Revolutionary War and composed of native English Tories.'" He also served as choir director and organist for many New York churches, such as St. George's Chapel (1854–60).

Besides his job with the Philharmonic, Bristow was associated full-time with the New York City public school system for many years, beginning in 1854. (According to the *American Art Journal* of Dec. 17, 1898, he was "assistant supervisor of music for the second district" [p. 163].) As late as 1889, the *American Musician* stated that "the choir of the Church of the Divine Paternity will be one of the best in New York after May 1 [1889]. That distinguished American musician and composer, Mr. George F. Bristow has been secured as director and organist ..." (vol. 13, no. 1, p. 14).

And in 1893 GEORGE HENRY CURTIS wrote: "Half a century of constant professional labor has not robbed [Bristow] of his intense devotion to his art.... [He] still walks his daily round of duty in the New York schools [and] attends to his weekly rehearsal as organist and conductor of a church choir..." (Curtis, p. 563).

Along with WILLIAM HENRY FRY, Bristow was an early champion of the American composer and resigned briefly from the Philharmonic in 1854 because it performed so few American works. According to the Dec. 4, 1880 issue of the *American Art Journal,* Bristow mingled "little in the society of the musical profession, and is rarely seen or heard of unless in the concerts of the Philharmonic. His home for many years has been in a quiet and unpretentious cottage in Morrisania [later a section of New York City's borough The Bronx]. Little would one think, when viewing it, that it was the cozy retreat of our illustrious composer" (vol. 36, no. 6, p. 109).

Rip Van Winkle, op. 22 (1855), was Bristow's only opera. It is built around Washington Irving's famous story. The opera was perhaps suggested by the example of *Ahmed al Kamel; or, The Pilgrim of Love* (1840), a drama-with-music by Charles E. Horn, based on Irving's *Tales of the Alhambra.* It was perhaps encouraged by the thousand-dollar prize offered by Ole Bull in Jan. 1855 for a new grand opera by an American based on an American subject. In any case, the libretto of *Rip Van Winkle* was the work of Jonathan Howard Wainwright, and the opera had seventeen performances in two months by the Pyne-Harrison English Opera Company at Niblo's Garden (Broadway and Prince Street) in New York commencing Sept. 27, 1855. (A reproduction of the playbill for the second performance may be found facing page 139 of Grenville Vernon's collection of songs *Yankee Doodle-doo,* New York: Payson & Clarke, 1927.) The opera consists of songs, duets, ensembles, and choruses interspersed with spoken dialogue. It received generally good, though mixed, reviews in the local newspapers, but the periodical *Musical Review and Gazette* thought that it should have been shortened by at least one half (vol. 6, no. 21, p. 334). George Henry Curtis stated many years later that he believed the opera would be the work "by which [Bristow] will be most tenderly remembered..." (Curtis, p. 559).

Rip Van Winkle was to be revived in Italian in 1865 by the impresario Max Maretzek but a fire destroyed the sets and costumes. It was staged, however, in Philadelphia in 1870 in English with the libretto revised by J. W. Shannon. A vocal score of this revised version was published by G. Schirmer in 1882. The excerpt in this anthology, taken from the 1882 Schirmer score, is from the opera's third (last) act. It is the aria sung by Rip after he wakes from his long sleep and returns to the changed Catskill mountain town he had previously known so well.

George Frederick Bristow
Photograph, date unknown

BIBLIOGRAPHY

George Frederick Bristow clipping file, Music Division, The New York Public Library.

Curtis, George Henry. "George Frederic [sic] Bristow." *Music* 3 (Mar. 1893), [547]–64.

Dictionary of American Biography. New York: Charles Scribner's Sons; London: Milford, 1928–37.

Mattfeld, Julius. *Variety Music Cavalcade 1620–1969.* 3rd ed. Englewood Cliffs, N.J.: Prentice-Hall, 1971.

The Message Bird 1:9 (Dec. 1, 1849), 149–50. (Bristow's song "I Would I Were a Favorite Flower" printed)

Odell, George C. D. *Annals of the New York Stage.* New York: Columbia University Press, 1927–49. (Vol. VI)

DUDLEY BUCK was born on Mar. 10, 1839 in Hartford, Conn. and died at Dudley Buck, Jr.'s home on Oct. 5, 1909 in Orange, N.J.—curiously enough, the same smallish city in which LOWELL MASON died in 1872. If JOHN KNOWLES PAINE became in 1861 upon his return from European studies "the leading organist in the United States" (Edwards, p. 123), he had stiff competition the next year from Buck, Paine's almost exact contemporary, upon *his* return from European studies. And while organ playing and composing church music faded as major activities from Paine's career, they remained primary with Buck until his retirement in 1903.

Paine became famous largely for his two symphonies, other large secular works, and his professorship at a prestigious Eastern university (Harvard); Buck was a virtuoso performer and secondarily a composer (though his obituary in *Musical America* of Oct. 16, 1909 claimed that his pieces were included on concert and choral programs more often "than those of any other American composer"—vol. 10, no. 23, p. 38).

The *Musical America* obituary also claimed that Buck achieved international fame not through his organ playing but with his cantata, *The Centennial Meditation of Columbus* (1876, poem by Sidney Lanier), commissioned for the opening of the Centennial Exposition. (For the same occasion, Paine was commissioned to compose a *Centennial Hymn,* poem by John Greenleaf Whittier.)

The interviewer, John William Black, stated in the Nov. 1901 issue of the magazine *Musical Life* that Buck's music was "pre-eminently practical" and his church music unique, "having its own pronounced qualities of attractiveness in formal outline, refinement in expression and charm of melodic and harmonic propriety" (vol. 1, p. 2).

Yes, it is certainly practical—and professional—and, like the anthem reprinted here, expressive. Though as a composer he is remembered mainly for his religious music, Buck did compose a few large secular works, among them an unpublished symphony, a Symphonic Overture—*Marmion* (after Sir Walter Scott), which was performed at least twice: Mar. 1878 and Mar. 1885—and two operas—*Deseret* (1880), a not very successful comedy on a Mormon theme with libretto by the New York journalist Augustus Crofutt (for which Buck was perhaps hoping for the success in light opera of his classmate in Leipzig, Arthur Sullivan), and the unproduced *Serapis.* (Hipsher gives the date for *Serapis* as "about 1888"; other sources give 1895.)

The libretto of *Serapis* was by Buck, "the subject . . . Egyptian," writes Hipsher on p. 98; "the time is the reign of Constantine; and the plot is woven about the dramatic destruction of the idol, *Serapis.*"

Upon the première of *Deseret*, the *New York Spirit of the Times* of Oct 30, 1880 noted that most of the audience "had evidently never been in a theatre before," loved the libretto, and found Buck's music "bright, strong, scholarly . . . not characteristic nor humorous" (unpaginated clipping in the Buck clipping file in the Music Division of The New York Public Library, hereafter referred to as the Buck Clipping File). (The contract between Buck and Crofutt may be found in the Music Division, The Library of Congress, call number: ML95.B9.)

Buck settled in Brooklyn in late 1875 or early 1876, where first he was organist/choirmaster at St. Ann's (Episcopal) Church, then at the Church of the Holy Trinity (1877–1902) ("after a service of twenty-two years at Holy Trinity he resigned . . . because of limitations set upon his selection of the music. . . . More than half the big choir followed him"—Buck's obituary in the *New York Sun,* Buck Clipping File); lastly he was at Plymouth Church (1902–03). He retired in the latter year.

Buck also helped form the all-male singing society the Apollo Club, which he conducted for decades (1877–1903).

Before the mid-1870s Buck as a young man studied composition and piano in Leipzig (like CHARLES PERKINS and WILLIAM MASON) with Moscheles and others, and organ in Dresden (1858–60) with Johann

Dudley Buck
Photograph, date unknown

Schneider, and lived in Paris for a year (1861–62). In the U.S.A. he was organist first in churches in Hartford (1862–67), where he married and fathered two children and published his first *Mottette Collection* (Boston: Ditson, 1864): "a work which marked an epoch in American church music"—Mathews, pp. 679–80.

Buck also began a fifteen-year series of touring appearances as a concert organist to show off the instruments of the organ builder William A. Johnson ("his organ-concert tours . . . exercised an influence that was important . . . in popularizing the best music throughout the country—in the small towns as well as in the larger cities"—*Dudley Buck,* [p. 1]). Like Theodore Thomas, Buck had a knack for mixing in his recitals the "popular" with the "classical," the light with the serious. (According to Mathews, p. 240, Buck had two special favorite crowd-pleasers: transcriptions of Wagner's *Tannhäuser* overture and Conradin Kreutzer's light *Night in Grenada* overture.)

After his parents' death, Buck moved to Chicago (1867–72), surviving the Great Fire of 1871 (he was performing in Albany at the time) but losing his house with its music room containing a three-manual organ, music scores brought back from Europe, and several of his own unfinished manuscripts. With insurance money obtained after the fire, he moved his family to Somerville, Mass. and his professional activities to Boston (1872–75). He worked in churches there, at the New England Conservatory, and eventually at the organ in the Boston Music Hall ("directly after the introduction of the great Boston organ, there began to be recitals every week upon it, and the young organists, such as Paine, Thayer, and Buck, vied with each other in rendering upon it the works of Bach . . ."—Mathews, p. 237).

Very significantly for Buck, it was apparently in Boston that he met or came to the attention of Theodore Thomas, who invited Buck in 1875 to become his assistant conductor at concerts in New York's Central Park Garden. Or perhaps it was in Cincinnati that the two men met: Buck was organist for the May festival there in 1875 and Thomas was the conductor. In any case, Buck came to New York "but the connection with the Thomas orchestra was soon terminated" (Mathews, p. 682). Thomas left New York for Chicago in 1878.

Buck's lovely *Rock of Ages,* op. 65, no. 3, was published in 1873, during his Boston years. The text, which first appeared in 1776, is by the English clergyman Augustus M. Toplady (1740–1778). It has been recorded on New World Records (NW-220), and for additional information on the piece, please see this author's liner notes on that recording.

BIBLIOGRAPHY

Dictionary of American Biography. New York: Charles Scribner's Sons; London: Milford, 1928–37.

Dudley Buck; A Complete Bibliography. New York: G. Schirmer [n.d.].

Edwards, George Thornton. *Music and Musicians of Maine.* Portland, Me.: The Southworth Press, 1928; reprinted New York: AMS Press, 1970; Da Capo, 1987.

Hipsher, Edward Ellsworth. *American Opera and Its Composers.* Philadelphia: Presser, 1927; New York: Da Capo, 1978.

Johnson, Frances Hall. *Musical Memories of Hartford.* Hartford: Witkover's, 1931; New York: AMS Press, [1970].

Mathews, W. S. B. *A Hundred Years of Music in America.* Chicago: Howe, 1889; New York: AMS Press, 1970.

The New York Times, Apr. 1, 1885, p. 5.

Odell, George C. D. *Annals of the New York Stage.* New York: Columbia University Press, 1927–49. (Vol. VIII)

The Organists' Journal 2 (Nov. 1890), 21.

GEORGE WHITEFIELD CHADWICK was born in Lowell, Mass. on Nov. 13, 1854 and died in Boston on Apr. 4, 1931. In his career as a student and teacher, he was associated with Boston's New England Conservatory of Music. He studied organ and harmony there in the early 1870s, taught at the school beginning in 1872, and served as its director from 1897 until his death. The buildings occupied by the school on Huntington Avenue were erected during his directorship.

Other than as an educator, he was highly regarded as the prolific composer of six concert overtures—beginning with his *Rip Van Winkle* (1879), composed as a graduation piece at the Leipzig Conservatory—three symphonies, seven operas and operettas, five string quartets, and numerous other works.

Around the turn of the century, movements from his second symphony, composed in 1885, and quartets were said to contain "jollity" and "themes of the plantation" (Elson, p. 174), which must have amused him. What they probably reflect is a Yankee openness and humor and perhaps the memory of the old church songs his relatives sang and the singing school tunes once taught by his father, an insurance man. Chadwick himself was named for the famous Methodist preacher George

Whitefield. The composer was one of two children, both boys, and his mother, as Carl Engel tells us, "died in giving birth to George" (Engel, p. 441).

Jubilee (1895), which has been called "the best known work of all the Chadwick literature" (Campbell, p. 136), is one of four character pieces—*Noël* (1895), *Hobgoblin* (1904), and *A Vagrom Ballad* (1896) are the others—which may be performed individually or together. If the latter, the title *Symphonic Sketches: Suite for Orchestra* is used. The composer said that his *Symphonic Sketches* were program music and that they might suggest a picture but that "everyone must make the picture for himself" (Detroit, p. 43). They were first performed as a unit on Nov. 21, 1904, in Jordan Hall at the New England Conservatory under Chadwick's direction. They are dedicated to Frederick S. Converse (1871–1940), Chadwick's colleague at the Conservatory, and were published in 1907.

Chadwick also said that *Jubilee* was in a simplified sonatina form, that it expressed an optimistic view of life, and that one of the themes was Southern in character. In the published score, the piece is preceded by a poem attributed by Chadwick to "D.R."; however, Dora J. Wilson, who has studied Chadwick's diaries, has suggested that the poem is probably by Chadwick himself (letter to this author; see below). The poem reads:

> No cool gray tones for me!
> Give me the warmest red and green,
> A cornet and a tamborine,
> To paint MY Jubilee!
>
> For when pale flutes and oboes play,
> To sadness I become prey;
> Give me the violets and the May,
> But no gray skies for me!

BIBLIOGRAPHY

Boston Symphony Orchestra, program notes (Feb. 7–8, 1908) [by Philip Hale?], 27th season, p. 1051.

Campbell, Douglas. *George W. Chadwick: His Life and Works*. Ph.D. dissertation, Eastman School of Music, University of Rochester, 1957. Rochester, N.Y.: University of Rochester Press, 1957.

Detroit Symphony Orchestra, program notes (Nov. 6, 1941) ["edited and prepared by Herman Wise"], 28th season, p. 43.

Dictionary of American Biography. New York: Charles Scribner's Sons; London: Milford, 1928–37.

Elson, Louis C. *The History of American Music*. Rev. ed. New York: Macmillan, 1915.

Engel, Carl. "George W. Chadwick." *Musical Quarterly* 10:3 (July 1924), 438–57.

Wilson, Dora J. Letter to the author, June 17, 1984.

EDWIN PEARCE CHRISTY, usually called Ned, was born on Nov. 28, 1815 in Philadelphia and died on May 21, 1862 in New York. He started a small blackface singing troupe in Buffalo, N.Y., in 1843 or 1844, one of the earliest known of such groups. He was very successful in the enterprise. He toured the show, became widely known, played New York, and retired there with a fortune early in 1855, barely a dozen years or so after he organized the group. About eight years later at the age of forty-six he jumped or fell from his second-floor bedroom window.

"Farewell Ladies" was registered for copyright in 1847, when the Christy Minstrels were in New York. It became better known, of course, in a slightly different form and under the title "Goodnight Ladies." The version reprinted here, however, is believed to be the first published edition of the famous song (see Fuld, p. 255). Claghorn in his *Biographical Dictionary of American Music* (p. 93) states that Christy is indeed the song's composer—and certainly it was published with Christy credited as composer. It is quite possible, though, that "Farewell Ladies" was composed by someone else, because it is known that pieces by other composers were published anonymously under the Christy banner or as by Christy himself. The most famous instance of the latter situation is the publication in 1851 of STEPHEN FOSTER's "Old Folks at Home" as "written and composed" by E. P. Christy. (Foster sold to Christy the permission to do this for the sum of $5.00.)

There was, in fact, quite a connection between Foster and Christy. After Foster's early minstrel pieces proved successful, he wrote to Christy, sent him several of the pieces, and suggested that they enter into an agreement by which Christy would have right of first refusal of all Foster's new songs; if he wished to première one of them, he would pay Foster ten dollars. This Christy agreed to. Then there was the famous letter of 1852 in which Foster tried (unsuccessfully) to buy back the right to have his own name on "Old Folks at Home." If Christy answered this, the letter has not been preserved; however, on the back of Foster's letter he wrote, "a vacillating skunk" (Chase, p. 294).

Christy also performed songs by the young GEORGE F. ROOT in his New York days, at a time when Root believed he could steal a bit of the popular market from Foster. The most successful of these were "Hazel Dell" (1853) and "Rosalie, the Prairie Flower" (1855).

He never personally took his group to England, but a "Christy's Minstrels" did play there in 1857, almost three years after his retirement. (George Harrington—one of the original members of the enterprise—who had taken the name Christy—carried on with the group after Edwin P. Christy retired.) The company was tremendously popular there, and as the Christy article in the *New Grove* dictionary points out, "Christy's Minstrels became the generic name for Negro minstrels in Great Britain."

BIBLIOGRAPHY

Chase, Gilbert. *America's Music, from the Pilgrims to the Present*. Rev. 2nd ed. New York: McGraw-Hill, 1966.

Claghorn, Charles Eugene. *Biographical Dictionary of American Music*. West Nyack, N.Y.: Parker, 1973.

Fuld, James. *The Book of World Famous Music*. 3rd ed., rev. and enlarged. New York: Dover, 1985.

Nathan, Hans. *Dan Emmett and the Rise of Early Negro Minstrelsy*. Norman, Okla.: University of Oklahoma Press, 1962, 2nd printing 1977.

Stevenson, Robert. "Edwin Pearce Christy." *The New Grove Dictionary of Music and Musicians* IV, 377. London: Macmillan Publishers, 1980.

GEORGE HENRY CURTIS was born in 1821 and died on Aug. 28, 1895 in Brooklyn, N.Y. His piece on Longfellow's poem *Endymion*, which he set as a part-song or secular anthem for male voices, was published as sheet music in New York in 1857. It was probably composed for and sung by a class at the fashionable all-male Brooklyn Collegiate and Polytechnic Institute, where Curtis was music instructor. A lithograph of the Institute is featured on the cover of the original edition. (The school began classes in Sept. 1855 as a liberal arts college but converted to a science and technology-only school at the turn of the century and changed its name slightly to Brooklyn Polytechnic Institute.) Curtis was apparently a busy itinerant teacher at the time *Endymion* was published, for he gave music instruction in at least six other New York schools.

A few years earlier he had taught at the New York Conservatory of Music (founded 1849) with William Bradbury (1816–1868) and his friend Francis Henry Nash, a singer.

Also in the year of 1857, Curtis was performed by the New York American Music Association, a concert group that featured American music, that was started by the composer Charles Jerome Hopkins (see the biographical sketch of his brother, JOHN HENRY HOPKINS, below) and supported by GOTTSCHALK, BRISTOW, WILLIAM MASON, and other musicians.

Curtis once described Bristow as "my life-long friend" (Curtis, p. 563), and he must have been at least acquainted with several other of the composers represented in this anthology. He and Bristow appeared together on the concert platform, and a line in the published vocal score of his cantata *Elutheria* (New York: Wm. Hall & Son, 1851) reads: "Copies of George F. Bristow's effective orchestral arrangement of this work may be obtained by one month's previous application to G. H. Curtis, 133 Varick Street, N.Y." This score also contains a list of about one hundred subscribers—persons who promised to buy at least one copy of the publication—among whom are W. J. WETMORE (and P. T. Barnum!).

Elutheria was conducted on at least three occasions by Bristow: at New York's Broadway Tabernacle in Apr. 1849 (Curtis, p. 551), in Brooklyn's Plymouth Church on Feb. 21, 1850 (*The Message Bird*, vol. 1, p. 250—whose review contained the following passage: "Both the writer [Horatio Stone] and composer deserve all praise and encouragement as Pioneers in the growth of native Music of a high order"), and in New York's Apollo Rooms on Apr. 25, 1851 (Odell, vol. VI, p. 95). (A review of the published vocal score of *Elutheria* appeared in the *Musical World*, vol. 3, p. 245.)

Among the composers represented in his school collection, *The Musical Monitor: A New Vocal Method for Schools*, are ALFRED PEASE and GEORGE WILLIAM WARREN (about one-fourth of the approximately 140 pieces in this collection are by Curtis himself). Curiously, he states in the book's preface that he intends the book for the use of the teacher "and *her* [emphasis mine] pupils in our schools"—he uses the feminine pronoun even though he himself was a teacher. Curtis concludes the preface rather charmingly by saying, "with a well grounded hope that the work may prove extensively useful, it is sent forth on its errand."

Another of his cantatas with text by a famous American literary figure—William Cullen Bryant—is *The Forest Melody*, which was performed at New York's Academy of Music on June 2, 1858 and at the Polytechnic Institute the next night.

In general, Curtis seems to have followed the lead of LOWELL MASON, seeing as how he was a school music teacher, an organist, and a compiler of tune books. (As a composer, he was, of course, more ambitious than Mason.) Other than *The Musical Monitor,* two of his books are *The Grammar School Vocalist* (1860) and *The Centennial School Singer; or, Songs of Patriotism and Peace* (1876), the latter for the "children of the American Union."

BIBLIOGRAPHY

The Brooklyn Daily Eagle, Fri., Aug. 30, 1895, p. 7 [Curtis' obituary].

Clippings on the Brooklyn Polytechnic Institute at the Brooklyn Historical Society, from the *Brooklyn Daily Eagle,* Thurs., Mar. 12, 1853 and *Newsweek,* Mar. 16, 1953.

Curtis, George Henry. "George Frederic [sic] Bristow." *Music* 3 (Mar. 1893), [547]–64.

The Message Bird 1:5 (Oct. 1849), 84; 1:15 (Mar. 1, 1850), 250.

The Musical Monitor: A New Vocal Method for Schools. New York: William A. Pond & Co., 1870.

The Musical World 3:16 (Apr. 15, 1852), 245.

The New York Musical World 18:346 (Nov. 14, 1857), 729 (this citation is for an advertising notice that also appeared in other issues of the magazine in 1857 and 1858).

Odell, George C. D. *Annals of the New York Stage.* New York: Columbia University Press, 1927–49.

AMBROSE DAVENPORT was born in Taunton, Mass. and died on July 24, 1906 in Norwood, a small town near Boston. Along with George Dutton, Jr., Davenport is easily the most shadowy figure represented in this anthology. He is not carried in any standard music or general biographical reference source, and is only fleetingly mentioned in one or two fairly obscure sources, such as *The American Musical Directory* (New York: Hutchinson, 1861). Information on Davenport has been pieced together largely from widely varying secondary sources, including the *Boston City Directory,* the card catalogs of at least two libraries, sheet music, one short magazine article, and circumstantial evidence.

That one article is in the Sept. 1890 issue of *The Folio* (vol. 35, no. 9, p. 329), the house organ of the Boston music publisher White-Smith. It accompanies a drawing of Davenport which adorns the cover. It states that he had been the editor of *The Folio* for the past three years, and after naming his birthplace adds that he was, however, "reared and educated in Boston." The article continues:

> he has been connected with the music business uninterruptedly since 1856. In 1865–66 he was a special contributor to the *Boston Musical Times,* and later was associated with his brother Mr. Warren Davenport, the well-known teacher of the voice, of Boston, as senior editor of the *Metronome.* . . . At the present time in addition to his duties as editor of *The Folio,* he is general supervisor of music engraving with the White-Smith Music Publishing Company.

Ambrose Davenport was probably a busy man, for in addition to the above activities he and Warren are listed in the Boston directory through 1866 as music engravers at 277 Washington Street (the address of the music publisher Oliver Ditson). In the 1867 directory their business address changes to 291 Washington (the address of the music publisher Henry Tolman).

In 1869 Ambrose and Warren formed their own company: Davenport Brothers, "music dealers and publishers" (as the directory described the company). (Davenport Brothers items may have been printed on the presses of White & Goulard and other Boston music publishers.) The directory listed the firm until 1887, when it either closed or changed hands.

Beginning in the 1881 directory, added to his association with Davenport Brothers, Warren Davenport is also a "vocal instructor" with a studio at 154 Tremont.

As he worked as engraver at the various Boston music publishers mentioned, Ambrose Davenport saw his compositions published by those houses. His anthem *Praise Ye the Lord,* included in this anthology, copyrighted in 1866, was brought out by Henry Tolman and Co. The title page of the piece lists it as part of the all-Davenport series *Praise Offerings for Morning and Evening Service.* This series consists of Davenport works numbered opus 1, 2, and 3. Each opus has two numbers: the piece here is op. 3, no. 1. (At the bottom of the last page of the anthem may be found the engraver's name: "W. Davenport.")

This piece is printed here not because it is an overlooked gem—the piece *is* forgotten but it is no gem—but because it is typical of its time (mid-19th century, high Victorian), place of composition and publication (big eastern U.S. city), and type (middle-class, or upper-middle-class, church anthem). For better or worse, churches in smaller towns would probably have taken it up or aped it, hence it is an artifact that not only reflects a certain taste but one that helped mold it as well. (There is known documentary evidence for the performance of the Davenport anthem, *Glory to God in the Highest* [1870], at Christmas 1880 in the Congregational Church, Auburndale, Mass. See the *American Art Journal,* vol. 34, no. 10 [Jan. 1881], p. 184.)

Besides the six anthems in the *Praise Offerings* series and the six-song cycle *Tone-Poems,* op. 4, other Davenport compositions include the anthem *Be Thou My Judge,* noted on a sheet-music cover, and the dozen songs and the eight hymns and choruses listed in the catalog of the Boston Public Library. Between that catalog and the New York Public Library's, there are also nine entries for his arrangements, editions, and translations. (Certainly, most curious of the arrangements are four vocal and instrumental quartet movements by Beethoven which Davenport scored for four voices and fitted with sacred texts and organ accompaniments.)

Ambrose Davenport's brief obituary notice in the *Boston Evening Transcript* (July 25, 1906, p. 10) states that he died "suddenly." If Warren Davenport grieved for the brother with whom he had worked for so many years, he did not have long to do so: Warren died a year and a half later on Jan. 3, 1908.

JAMES MONROE DEEMS was born on Jan. 5, 1818 in Baltimore and died there on Apr. 18, 1901. As a child, he performed in the band conducted by his father, Jacob Deems, who had been a captain in the War of 1812, and was considered a child prodigy. Before he travelled to Dresden to study music with J. F. Dotzauer in 1839, Deems played the bugle, clarinet, French horn, piano, and organ. (He had studied privately with George Loder in Baltimore before travelling to Europe.) Deems returned to Baltimore in 1841 and opened a studio.

Beginning in the 1830s or 40s in Baltimore, Deems was acquainted with the young German-American musician HENRY DIELMAN. For ten years (1848–58) Deems taught music at the University of Virginia and also composed.

On Nov. 21, 1857 the music critic of the *New York Musical World,* reviewing a concert of the short-lived New York American Music Association, wrote: "A selection was given from an oratorio entitled *Nebuchadnezzar,* by Mr. J. Deems. Mr. Deems is an American, living in Virginia. He has studied in Germany, we understand, under Romberg, the composer of Schiller's *Song of the Bell.* Other compositions, such as songs, etc. have already emanated from the same composer, which have been published. The oratorio . . . is a work of decided merit" (vol. 18, no. 347, p. 723). (The magazine's information that Deems studied with the composer of Schiller's *Song of the Bell* [1808] is incorrect; its composer, Andreas Romberg [1767–1821], died eighteen years before Deems travelled to Europe.)

In 1861 Deems raised the First Maryland Cavalry, beginning with the rank of Major. He saw much action during the Civil War, including the battle at Gettysburg, and emerged a Brigadier General. Back in Baltimore in 1863—rheumatism forced his resignation from the army—Deems performed on the bugle at the newish Franklin Square Baptist Church (founded 1854) and remained a faithful member of that church until his death. He also taught music privately and composed.

The Peabody Institute had been founded in the early spring of 1857 but the first concert there was not given until Dec. 22, 1866. Deems and three others conducted the orchestra for the first season of eight concerts. Deems was the sole conductor during the season 1867–68. LUCIEN SOUTHARD was appointed the first head of Peabody's music department and conductor of its orchestra in the Fall of 1868. When Southard was replaced in 1871, Harry Deems, James Deems's son and a local music teacher, was considered for the job.

James Deems left a finished opera, *Esther,* an unfinished one, *The Unbidden Guest,* the oratorio already mentioned, and a number of songs. "May I Hope to Call Thee Friend" (1844), reproduced in this anthology, was apparently his first published song.

The word "cornopean," now used only as the name of a loud reed stop on a pipe organ, was primarily used by the British until about the middle of the 19th century to identify the early cornet. Deems played this instrument. For modern performance, a woodwind, such as a clarinet or oboe, might replace the cornet.

"May I Hope to Call Thee Friend" is cited by William Treat Upton as "giving evidence of real ability and musicianship" (Upton, p. 51).

BIBLIOGRAPHY

History of Baltimore, Maryland. [Baltimore?]: S. B. Nelson, 1898.

Keefer, Lubov. *Baltimore's Music: The Haven of the American Composer.* Baltimore: Printed by J. H. Furst, 1962.

Musical Courier 42:18 (Wed., May 1, 1901), 26 [Deems's obituary].

Robinson, Ray Edwin. *A History of the Peabody Conservatory of Music.* D. Music Education dissertation, Indiana University, 1969. Ann Arbor, Mich.: University Microfilms, 1969.

Stephenson, Kurt. *Andreas Romberg*. Hamburg: Hans Christians, 1938.

Upton, William Treat. *Art-Song in America: A Study in the Development of American Music*. Boston: Ditson, 1930; reprinted with Supplement, New York: Johnson Reprint, [1969].

HENRY DIELMAN was born on Apr. 26, 1811 in Frankfurt, Germany, and died on Oct. 12, 1882, in Emmitsburg, Md. His full name was John Casper Henry Dielman, but apparently he preferred to use only Henry. He came from an artistic family. His father, John Casper Dielman (maybe the composer was called Henry at home), was also a musician; two brothers were artists—J. Fürchtegot (1804–1885) and Johannes (1819–1866); three cousins also distinguished themselves in art—Jacob Dielman as a painter, Francis Dielman as a lithographer, and Jean Dielman as a sculptor. Henry was musically precocious, playing the flute and violin before he was eleven. His mother and musician father saw to it that he had excellent musical instruction in Frankfurt and also in the town of Offenbach.

In 1828, when he was seventeen years old, he went to Philadelphia to play violin in the orchestra of the Chestnut Street Theatre. He had been recruited by a Mr. Wepfer who had been sent to Germany by the theater manager and actor William Warren (1767–1832). (Mr. Wepfer was supposed to bring home a *corps de ballet* but, instead, he brought five instrumentalists!) At that time, the management of the Chestnut Street Theatre shifted from Warren to Francis Courtney Wemyss (1797–1889) and Lewis T. Pratt, who also managed a theater in Baltimore and one in Washington, D.C. Dielman's solo recital debut was apparently in Baltimore in Nov. 1828.

While in Philadelphia, he composed several pieces, including an overture for orchestra, but he did not become widely known or prominent as a composer during his career. He stayed in Philadelphia for about two years, then took up residence in Baltimore for almost fourteen (with apparently about two years spent in Washington, D.C. during the latter period). In Baltimore, which had a prominent German community, he was leader of the orchestra at Wemyss and Pratt's Holliday Street Theatre, and he formed the Baltimore Musical Association, an amateur group that presented concerts. He taught music privately and directed the music at several churches, including the Catholic cathedral (St. John's), St. Vincent's, Zion, and the Protestant-Episcopal Christ's Church. He also married Emily Dawson, a daughter of Philemon Dawson, captain of the English Merchant Marine. Dielman and Emily had four daughters and a son.

In 1843, when he was thirty-two years old, he accepted an offer from Mount St. Mary's College in Emmitsburg, Md., to be professor of music and organist. At the well-thought-of, all-male college near the Pennsylvania border, WILLIAM HENRY FRY and his brothers, Joseph and Edward, had all been students fifteen years before Dielman began teaching there.

In 1849 Georgetown University in Washington, D.C., conferred upon him an honorary Doctor of Music degree, and it was presented to him by the President of the United States of the time, Zachary Taylor. As far as is known, Dielman was the first to receive such a degree from an American university (LOWELL MASON was the second, receiving the degree from New York University in 1855).

Sometime later, about 1880, the Archbishop of Baltimore, James Cardinal Gibbons, asked Dielman to return to the city and assume responsibility for the Cathedral choir—a prestigious post. But Dielman was apparently so pleased with his situation at Mount St. Mary's that he declined the offer.

The undated original edition of the glee *Bee's Wings and Fish* was published in Baltimore probably in the 1830s shortly after the youthful Dielman became a resident there. (The "bee's wings" of the title refer to shiny scales of tartar formed in port and other wines that are kept for a long time.) He saw another glee, "There Are Three Cheering Stars of Light," published in the 1834 collection *Six Original Glees*. Other than the orchestral overture he composed in Philadelphia in the late 1820s, he wrote anthems, masses, and other church music, and band marches for the inaugurations of presidents Jackson, Harrison, and Taylor.

BIBLIOGRAPHY

Baltimore 1729–1929, 200th Anniversary. [Baltimore?]: *Baltimore Municipal Journal*, 1929.

Henry Dielman clipping file in Music Division, The New York Public Library.

History of Baltimore, Maryland. [Baltimore?]: S. B. Nelson, 1898.

Keefer, Lubov. *Baltimore's Music: The Haven of the American Composer*. Baltimore: Printed by J. H. Furst, 1962.

GEORGE DUTTON, JR. was born before 1825 presumably in Philadelphia or in Utica, N.Y., where his family lived beginning in 1821. He moved to the "big" city of Rochester, N.Y., 133 miles from Utica on the Erie Canal, just completed in 1820. Dutton's sister, Sarah, was living in Rochester, the wife of the Rev. J. H. McIlvaine, minister of that city's First Presbyterian Church.

Readily obtainable information on Dutton begins with the Rochester City Directory for 1844, in which he is listed as an "attorney, etc." The Dutton piano piece reprinted here, *The Wood Pigeon*, was published nine years earlier in 1835 by G. P. Reed & Co. of Boston.

In the Rochester directories for 1845–46 through 1857–58, George Dutton, Jr. is listed as the proprietor of a music store; full-page advertisements appear for his "Music Rooms," located variously at 12 Buffalo (2nd story) (1845–46), 27 State (1847–52), 83 Main (1853–56), and 36 North (1857–58). The store sold pianos, other musical instruments, and sheet music; the Dutton advertisement for 1845–46 also mentioned "instruction in music, for a small class of piano scholars." (One wonders how many piano scholars responded?)

The Rochester directory for 1859 listed him as "Rev. George Dutton." However, there was an advertisement for the Dutton music store. No directory was published for 1860. There is no mention of him or the music store in subsequent Rochester directories. An item in Rochester's newspaper *Union and Advertiser* of Feb. 10, 1859 mentioned that Dutton had received his license as a Presbyterian minister. M. M. Bagg, in his 1877 *The Pioneers of Utica: Being Sketches of Its Inhabitants and Institutions . . .* (Utica: Curtiss & Childs, 1877), merely states of Dutton that he was "first a music dealer, afterwards a Presbyterian minister," and "is deceased" (p. 525).

Bagg has much more to say about the remarkable George Dutton, Sr. (1789–1854), who moved to Utica from Philadelphia in 1821 as a piano salesman, and in that year sold "the first piano that was sold in the village" (p. 524). Dutton, Sr. knew Thomas Hastings (1784–1872), LOWELL MASON's haughty, eminent friend—a resident of Utica between 1823 and 1832.

George Dutton, Jr., was from something of a musical family, for not only did his father compose, perform, and conduct (church choirs and small orchestras), but his brother William H. Dutton (1820–1904) was also a composer, performer, and conductor, being associated with the Utica Musical Society until he left Utica in 1865.

George Dutton, Jr., composed at least three vocal works (which are at NYPL) and a dozen piano pieces other than *The Wood Pigeon*. He was a "grass-roots" composer who never studied in or resided in a very large urban center such as New York, Boston, or Philadelphia.

BIBLIOGRAPHY

Cuda, Rebecca Ann, of the Reference Dept. of the Utica (N.Y.) Public Library. Letter to the author, June 13, 1984.

"Death of William H. Dutton." *Utica Daily Press,* July 22, 1904, p. 5 [William H. Dutton's obituary].

Emrich, Carol, of the Rochester (N.Y.) Public Library, Local History Division. Letter to the author, Nov. 9, 1984.

The National Union Catalog/Pre-1956 Imprints. 731 vols. London: Mansell Information/Publishing, 1968–81.

Union and Advertiser (Rochester, N.Y.), Dec. 22, 1854, p. 3 [notice of George Dutton, Sr.'s death].

"Was a Native of Utica." *Utica Daily Press,* Nov. 29, 1920 (Monday morning) [William Dalliba Dutton's obituary; he was the son of William H. Dutton].

STEPHEN ALBERT EMERY was born in Paris, Me. on Oct. 4, 1841 and died in Boston on Apr. 15, 1891. He studied music in Portland (Maine), Leipzig, and Dresden. Most of his music (about 150 pieces in all) was composed at Boston's New England Conservatory of Music, where he taught harmony and piano from the school's beginning in 1867 until his death. He also taught theory and composition at Boston University. Emery was a teacher of the composers Horatio Parker, Henry Hadley, Ethelbert Nevin, and many others.

Emery is remembered chiefly for his songs and piano pieces and his popular text books *Elements of Harmony* (Boston, 1879), which has been described as filling a role in American music as "Webster's spelling book was to [American] letters" (Hughes, p. 95), and *Foundation Studies in Pianoforte Playing* (Boston, 1882). He was also an editor of the periodical the *Musical Herald*.

Emery's piano piece *Crystal Spring* was published in 1860 (when the composer was nineteen); his European studies commenced in 1862.

BIBLIOGRAPHY

Dictionary of American Biography. New York: Charles Scribner's Sons; London: Milford, 1928–37.

Hughes, Rupert. *Contemporary American Composers.* Boston: L. C. Page and Co., 1900.

DANIEL DECATUR EMMETT was born on Oct. 29, 1815 in Mount Vernon, Ohio and died there on June 28, 1904. He is famous as the probable inventor of the blackface minstrel show and, of course, as composer of the much-reprinted "Dixie" (composed in 1859 for Bryant's Minstrels, published in 1860). With three friends he formed the troupe they called the Virginia Minstrels and gave the first full-length blackface show in Boston in Mar. 1843. The song "Ole Dan Tucker" was part of that show.

Emmett is author of the words (he said he wrote them in 1830 or 31), but the jaunty tune is apparently of uncertain origin, though Emmett claimed he was the composer. Whatever the origin—perhaps it is a folk tune—it is certainly native American with its running fiddle lines and syncopation, as is Emmett's earthy dialect text. It was a popular tune for decades and used for campaign songs, such as "Our Flag Is Up" (1848), and for the Hutchinson Family's anti-slavery song "Get Off the Track" (1848).

Archie Green's article, cited fully below, mentions the many period publications of the song, ruminates on the persona of Dan Tucker as revealed in the text, and gives important notes about the song. Apparently Green assumes that Emmett composed the music, too: his article neither denies nor asserts the fact.

Before 1843 Emmett travelled with circuses and did a brief hitch in the U.S. Army as a fifer in 1835. Between 1858 and 1866 he worked for Bryant's minstrel troupe in New York as writer of songs and performer (banjo and probably fiddle and other instruments). From the later 1860s through the 1880s he lived in Chicago, and finally moved back to his birthplace in Ohio and died there a poverty-stricken old man.

BIBLIOGRAPHY

Chase, Gilbert. *America's Music, from the Pilgrims to the Present.* Rev. ed. New York: McGraw-Hill, 1966.

Dictionary of American Biography. New York: Charles Scribner's Sons; London: Milford, 1928–37.

Green, Archie. "Old Dan Tucker." *JEMF Quarterly* 17 (Summer 1981), 85–86, 94, 106.

Nathan, Hans. *Dan Emmett and the Rise of Early Negro Minstrelsy.* Norman, Okla.: University of Oklahoma Press, 1962, 2nd printing 1977.

PETER ERBEN was born in Philadelphia, Pa. ca. 1770 and died in Brooklyn, N.Y. on Apr. 30, 1861. Very little is known about this church musician-composer-publisher beyond his dates and the fact that he was father of the prominent New York organ-builder Henry Erben (1800–1884). The following few facts about his career were derived from the books of Wolfe, Messiter, and Claghorn (cited below) and from conversations with Vera Brodsky Lawrence of New York City, who generously shared information of many kinds with me.

Erben's career apparently centered around New York's Episcopalian Trinity Church and the other churches of Trinity Parish. In 1800 he was director of a group known as the Society of Cultivating Church Music, which was associated with Trinity Church, and between 1820 and 1839 was the church's organist. He retired in the latter year and was buried from that church twenty-two years later.

From at least 1811 (and maybe as early as 1807) until 1815, Erben was organist of St. George's Chapel (now Church). He was also organist at St. John's in 1813 and at St. Mark's in the Bowery during 1824 and 1825. (These three chapels or churches were in Trinity Parish.)

Wolfe records that as a music publisher Erben issued seventeen pieces of sheet music up to 1820. Erben's own collection *Select Psalm and Hymn Tunes* was published by him in 1806, though the publication date of his *Hymn for Whitsunday,* reproduced in this anthology, is unknown (Wolfe has it as 1819 [?]).

Before and after his retirement as an organist, Erben may have helped his son build organs. In the New York Directory for 1843 he is listed as an "organ manufacturer." Wolfe states that Erben may have helped his son construct the organ that was installed in Trinity Church in 1842.

BIBLIOGRAPHY

Claghorn, Charles Eugene. *Biographical Dictionary of American Music.* West Nyack, N.Y.: Parker, 1973.

Messiter, Arthur Henry. *A History of the Choir and Music of Trinity Church, New York, from Its Organization to the Year 1897.* New York: Edwin S. Gorham, 1906; New York: AMS Press, 1970.

Wolfe, Richard J. *Secular Music in America, 1801–1825: A Bibliography.* 3 vols. New York: The New York Public Library, 1964.

CARYL FLORIO was the pseudonym of William James Robjohn, who was born in Tavistock, Devon, England on Nov. 2 (not Nov. 3 as stated in *Baker's Biographical Dictionary* and other standard biographical sources), 1843 and died in Morgantown, N.C. on Nov. 21, 1920. From known facts, circumstantial evidence, and hopefully knowledgeable assumptions, the following account has been deduced of Robjohn's family and early years in the United States.

He was brought as a youngster by his English parents to New York about 1858. (Though both were English, Robjohn's parents met and were married when on trips to the U.S.A.) The father, also named William, a mechanic-inventor and organ builder, joined his elder brother, Thomas Robjohn, who had immigrated to the U.S.A. in the 1830s, in the organ-building business. The move was also occasioned, perhaps mainly, by the touch of consumption developed by the young William James Robjohn, for which a doctor said the only cure was a sea voyage; and sure enough, the trip did the trick.

The Robjohn brothers eventually left their independent business, however, and worked full-time for two other brothers, John and Caleb Odell, who ran a flourishing organ-building concern that lasted for a hundred years, beginning in 1859. Florio-Robjohn later wrote that his "father remained with the Odells until the time of his death" (Robjohn materials, p. 31). (For accounts of the Robjohn brothers see Cameron and Ogasapian.)

Meanwhile, the young William James Robjohn became the first boy soloist at New York's Trinity Church and after about a year and a half moved briefly to Elmira, N.Y. (His parents apparently stayed in Elmira for several years.) He subsequently had various jobs as organist and choirmaster (Ellinwood lists a W. J. Robjohn as assistant organist in Trinity Parish until 1863 — Appendix A, p. 187), and settled permanently in America. Young Robjohn toured as an actor between 1862 and 1868, met GEORGE F. ROOT in Chicago, and worked at the Root & Cady music store there. He assumed the pseudonym Caryl Florio in 1870. In later years he wrote that according to his aunt (Thomas Robjohn's wife), "I was 'disgracing the family name' and doing general social damage to all who had the misfortune of being related to me. So to save 'the family name' I abandoned it" (Robjohn materials, pp. 37–38).

He composed much: church anthems and a few hymns (he was "especially known for his hymns," said, probably incorrectly, the second of his obituaries cited below); a piano trio (1866); four string quartets (1872–96); a piano concerto in A-flat (1875–86); the light opera

Caryl Florio
(William James Robjohn)
Photograph, date unknown

Mercury's Tricks (1869); at least two grand operas (*Gulda,* 1879, and *Uncle Tom's Cabin,* performed in Philadelphia in 1882); and two symphonies (both 1887).

After the failure of *Uncle Tom's Cabin* in its one presentation and the lukewarm critical reception of an all-Robjohn concert in New York on Mar. 27, 1888, Robjohn composed little (and what he did compose lacked the inspiration and spirit of his earlier work). The Mar. 27, 1888 concert, financed by Robjohn, featured Theodore Thomas and his orchestra and included the two symphonies (the second an orchestration of his first string quartet), the piano concerto, and two songs.

For five years beginning in 1896 (his obituary in *The New York Times,* cited below, erroneously stated 1891), Robjohn was something of a *Kapellmeister*—rather like Haydn at Esterhazy—being in charge of the music at Biltmore, George Vanderbilt's estate near Asheville, N.C. After returning to New York for the period 1901 through June 1903, he returned to the Asheville area as a choirmaster and teacher, remaining there until his death at the age of seventy-seven.

Robjohn's works for saxophone—all unpublished during his lifetime—include a quintet for four saxophones and piano, and a work for saxophone solo and chamber orchestra, as well as the quartet of 1879, which is published here for the first time. These works were composed for and performed by the Dutch-born Edward A. Lefêbre (1834[?]–1911), a saxophone virtuoso, who is credited with introducing the instrument not only to the United States but to Holland, Denmark, Sweden, Germany, and Cape Town, South Africa (*American Art Journal*, vol. 39, no. 1, p. 3). Lefêbre came to the U.S.A. in 1871 as first clarinetist in the orchestra of the Parepa-Rosa English Opera Company. He also played saxophone in P. S. Gilmore's Twenty-second Regiment Band.

At a concert of Florio's works at New York's Chickering Hall on a rainy Apr. 29, 1880, Lefêbre and three other players gave a performance of the 1879 quartet. The periodical *Musical Review* (vol. 2, no. 4, p. 43) described the number of the audience as "respectable" despite the bad weather and, referring to the quartet as *Allegro de concert*, said the work "was a brisk and refreshing introduction to the concert and was greeted with enthusiastic applause" (p. 44). The review (p. 43) identified the saxophonists, other than Lefêbre, as Franz Walrabe, Henry Steckelberg, and William F. Schultz. We have used the above title for the work herein, retaining his working title on the manuscript as a subtitle.

Though on Apr. 28, 1883 in the article cited above the *American Art Journal* could state that "the saxophone has long been one of the favorite instruments in Europe, and is fast becoming so in America," Robjohn's prominent use of the instrument around that time seems to be the major evidence of such popularity in this country. The same article in the *American Art Journal* also reported that the instrument "gives that exquisitely pure, full, soft tone so pleasing to the true musician" (well, not to all "true" musicians: Rossini referred to its sound as "the most beautiful tone paste that I know" ["la plus belle pâte de son que je connaisse"]—Saxophone clipping file, Music Division, The New York Public Library). The magazine's statement that the saxophone had "long been one of the favorite instruments in Europe" could be debated also. Though it was patented in the 1840s by the Belgian instrument maker Adolphe Sax (1814–1894), only Meyerbeer, Auber, and perhaps a few other composers had written it into several of their scores; Berlioz spoke well of it, and Bizet wrote for it. Much later Richard Strauss would use it in his *Symphonia Domestica* (1904) and Ravel in his *Bolero* (1928). The evidence of its popularity by 1883 is not exactly overwhelming. In the U.S.A., saxophones were common in circus bands by 1895 (Parkinson, p. 13).

Lefêbre organized the New York Saxophone Quartet Club (or the Wonder Quartette, as it was also billed) around 1879. Stating the staggeringly obvious, the same 1883 article in the *American Art Journal* remarked about the Lefêbre group: "one serious obstacle was the comparatively small number of compositions existing for such a quartet" (p. 3). Enter Florio-Robjohn. The article continued: "good fortune brought the Club to the notice of [Florio], a most talented musician, well known as a pianist and organist of great merit and"—it added—"a charming composer" (p. 3).

BIBLIOGRAPHY

American Art Journal 48:25 (Apr. 7, 1888), 388. (Review of the all-Robjohn concert Mar. 27, 1888.)

Cameron, Peter T. "A Chronology of the Organ Builders Working in New York City," p. 84 in *Bicentennial Tracker*. [Wilmington, Ohio?]: The Organ Historical Society, 1976.

Cantrell, Barton. "William James Robjohn" in *The New Grove Dictionary of Music and Musicians*, XVI, 77. London: Macmillan Publishers, 1980.

Ellinwood, Leonard. *The History of American Church Music*. New York: Morehouse-Gorham, 1953; New York: Da Capo, 1970.

Messiter, A. H. *A History of the Choir and Music of Trinity Church, New York*. New York: Edwin S. Gorham, 1906; New York: AMS Press, 1970.

The New York Times. Mon., Nov. 1920, p. 15 [Robjohn's obituary].

Norwood, Wally. *Adolphe Sax, 1814–1894, His Life and Legacy*. Bramley, Hampshire: Bramley Books, 1980.

Ogasapian, John. *Organ Building in New York City: 1700–1900*. Braintree, Mass.: The Organ Literature Foundation, 1977.

Parkinson, Thomas P. "Circus Music." *The Sonneck Society Newsletter* 9 (Spring 1983), 13, 14.

Robjohn, William James. [*Biographical Sketch*] [a Robjohn obituary from an unidentified newspaper. Library of Congress catalog number: ML410.R25].

———. *Materials for an Autobiographical Sketch of Caryl Florio, Musician*. [Transcribed by Barton Cantrell] Unpublished. Music Division, The New York Public Library.

Root, George Frederick. *The Story of a Musical Life: An Autobiography*. Cincinnati: The John Church Co., 1891; New York: Da Capo, 1970.

BIOGRAPHICAL SKETCHES: Foster

STEPHEN COLLINS FOSTER was born in Lawrenceville (now a neighborhood of Pittsburgh), Pa. on July 4, 1826 and died in New York on Jan. 13, 1864. As a youngster he briefly attended three schools in Pennsylvania—Athens Academy (Tioga Point), Towanda Academy (Towanda), and Jefferson College (Canonsburg)—but his formal training, especially in music, was scant.

He worked as an office clerk and bookkeeper in Pittsburgh and Cincinnati between 1846 and 1850, marrying Jane MacDowell in June of the latter year. During the next decade, he achieved his greatest success as a songwriter; he and Jane had a daughter, Marion, in 1851; he buried his parents and at least one other close family member; and he lived apart from his family for long stretches of time. In 1860 he moved to New York and died there four years later in Bellevue Hospital.

Foster was essentially a very gifted amateur who "hit it big" as a writer of minstrel songs just at a time when the blackface troupes were needing so much music. Along with many other songwriters of the day he turned out quasi-art songs, popular ballads, patriotic and novelty songs—many of them distinguished by marvelous melodies. The texts, some by Foster himself, are invariably wistful or sad. He produced about 189 songs in all and a handful of instrumental pieces and arrangements. Some of the songs became so popular and widely known that many people assumed they were of folk origin. They were also influential.

For a long time said to mirror elements of black music, Foster's songs seem more to demonstrate the influence of Irish and Scotch tunes which were so popular here, especially during the publication between 1808 and 1834 of *Irish Melodies* by the Irish poet and songwriter Thomas Moore (1779–1852). But today, Foster's music is regarded as typically American the world over. There have been more books and articles written about him than any other American composer. His complete works were published in facsimile by Josiah K. Lilly in 1933.

As far as is known, Foster was America's first professional songwriter. No person is known before or during Foster's time to have made his or her living at songwriting alone, as Foster did after he was about twenty-three or twenty-four.

His "Oh! Susanna" is a classic American popular song. It was first performed in 1847 by a local singing group in Pittsburgh's Eagle Ice Cream Saloon and first published in 1848. It was used by Edwin P. Christy's minstrel troupe and others in New York and on tour. It is written in a supposedly authentic "darky" dialect and is in the verse-chorus form favored by the minstrel troupes. It was adopted as a kind of theme song by the "49ers" who travelled to California to find gold in 1849.

John Tasker Howard, who contributed importantly to the Foster literature with the biography *Stephen Foster, America's Troubadour*, considered, however, that "Oh! Susanna" was indebted to the earlier minstrel song "Gwing Long Down," published in 1844 and attributed to DANIEL EMMETT (*Our American Music*, 4th ed., p. 181). And, indeed, the tunes of the two songs are somewhat similar. But "Oh! Susanna" is stamped with a kind of originality, merriment, and creativity that make it unique among American popular songs.

BIBLIOGRAPHY

Austin, William W. *"Susanna," "Jeanie," and "The Old Folks at Home."* New York: Macmillan, 1975.

Hamm, Charles. *Yesterdays: Popular Song in America.* New York: Norton, 1979.

Howard, John Tasker. *Our American Music: A Comprehensive History from 1620 to the Present.* 4th ed. New York: Crowell, 1965.

——. *Stephen Foster, America's Troubadour.* New York: Crowell, 1934; new ed. 1953.

Stephen Foster
Left, with George Cooper (1840–1927);
photograph from either late 1863 or early 1864,
about two weeks before Foster's death

WILLIAM HENRY FRY was born on Aug. 10, 1813 (not 1815 as stated in the *Dictionary of American Biography*) in Philadelphia, Pa. and died on Dec. 21, 1864 in Santa Cruz, West Indies. He is famous as being the composer of the first produced American grand opera: *Leonora*, performed June 4, 1845 at Philadelphia's Chestnut Street Theatre. The libretto—in English, of course—was written by William Fry's brother Joseph Reese Fry (1811–1865), based on a dramatized version of Edward Bulwer-Lytton's novel *The Lady of Lyons*. The libretto was translated into Italian and the score revised for a New York production in Mar. 1858. A piano-vocal score of the first version was published (New York, Philadelphia: E. Ferrett & Co., 1846), as was an Italian-English libretto of the second (Philadelphia: P. E. Abel, 1858). Receiving a mixed critical reception and never wildly successful, *Leonora* was cast in a highly Italianate mold. Fry apparently thought (as did other Americans) that since opera was born and shaped in Italy, all operas should then reflect this. The critic Richard Grant White wrote of *Leonora* twenty-four years after its New York première that "on the whole" it was "much admired" there, "some of its airs became popular," and that its composer, "with encouragement and time" could "produce something of which musical Americans might have been proud. But he did not have the encouragement, nor yet time . . ." (White, p. 202).

Fry's prominent, one-eyed, newspaper-publisher father, William Fry (1777–1855)—he founded the Philadelphia *National Gazette* in 1820—saw to it that William Henry Fry had private composition instruction from Paris-born Leopold Meignen (1793–1873). The three eldest Fry brothers—William Henry (as director and possible arranger), Joseph (as translator), and Edward (1815–1889, as stage manager)—produced Bellini's opera *Norma* in English in Philadelphia on Jan. 11, 1841. It was William Henry's closest exposure to opera prior to the composition of *Leonora*.

In 1846 (the year after *Leonora*'s première), Fry left for Europe. Between that year and 1850, he travelled (settling in Paris by Dec. 1849) as foreign correspondent for the *New-York Tribune* and Philadelphia *Ledger*. (The Dec. 1849 date is from p. 52 of Upton's far-from-satisfactory biography of Fry.) While there he tried but failed to interest the Paris Opera in performing *Leonora* at his own expense. (On p. 21 in the book *Crotchets and Quavers*, Max Maretzek, who was associated at one time with Edward Fry, erroneously maintains that the sole purpose of William Henry Fry's trip was to recruit singers who would be willing to perform *Leonora* in New York.)

William Henry Fry
From a daguerreotype, date unknown

Fry remained in Paris until Oct. 1852, and may have met Hector Berlioz and LOUIS MOREAU GOTTSCHALK (sixteen years his junior), though Fry was not in Paris (if Upton is correct in his dates) at the time of Gottschalk's public debut on Apr. 17, 1849. Both he and Gottschalk returned to the United States on the mail steamship *Humbolt*, but Fry was on a slightly earlier sailing, arriving in New York on Nov. 11, 1852. Gottschalk arrived on Jan. 10, 1853. Certainly Fry's review of a Gottschalk recital (quoted on pp. 267–68 of the Fry biography by Upton) is gentle and laudatory, and offers non-technical, friendly advice.

Fry returned to New York to be an editor and music critic of Horace Greeley's *New-York Tribune*. Two days after arriving in New York, Fry embarked on an ambitious series of ten lectures, long planned, entitled History and Esthetics of Music, "illustrated" by the Philharmonic, a military band, vocal soloists from two visiting Italian opera companies, and a huge chorus—all conducted by GEORGE FREDERICK BRISTOW! There was an added (eleventh) lecture, and the series is said to have lost about $4,000 (Upton, p. 123). As a lecturer, Fry apparently was brilliant, eccentric, and long-winded.

Throughout his adult life, Fry seldom missed an opportunity to propagandize for the American composer and for American music.

Notre-Dame of Paris, completed in 1863, was Fry's third opera (though he worked earlier on other, incomplete ones) and his last completed work. All but the last scene, however, was composed a year earlier in 1862. The libretto, again by Joseph Reese Fry, based on the novel *Notre-Dame de Paris* (1831)—later known in the English-speaking world as *The Hunchback of Notre Dame*—by Victor Hugo (1802–1885), omits many scenes and characters from the original. Gone, for instance, is the entire episode of Esmeralda branded as a witch, so prominent in the novel.

Since neither the score nor libretto was ever published complete—the excerpt included here is from the privately printed (1864) vocal score of the first act—I will give a brief résumé of the opera's plot. The action takes place in 15th-century Paris. Told in four acts, the story is basically of the dancing girl Esmeralda (Fry was apparently going to name the opera after her but then changed his mind and used an English translation of Hugo's original title) and the three men who love her: Phoebus de Chateaupers (Captain of the Royal Guard), called simply Chateaupers throughout the opera, who is loved in return by Esmeralda; Quasimodo's guardian, Don Frollo; and Quasimodo himself, the deformed bell-ringer of the cathedral. Esmeralda's long-lost mother, here called Gudule—also a leading character—is finally revealed to her daughter. Esmeralda is accused of murdering Chateaupers (though Frollo is guilty) and is eventually hanged (though Chateaupers does not actually die until after her hanging!). Frollo is prevented by Chateaupers from stabbing Quasimodo who then stabs Frollo and himself. As can be seen, the Frys changed Hugo's events and characters somewhat and added melodrama to a novel that was melodramatic on its own terms. (A detailed synopsis of the complicated libretto may be found in Upton, pp. 168–70.)

The scene included in this anthology contains music for all the major characters except Gudule (the excerpt is no. 8 in the vocal score). The chorus hails Quasimodo who has been crowned the current King of Fools in an annual ceremony of the Parisian commoners.

The opera's première—it was conducted by young Theodore Thomas—was held at Philadelphia's Academy of Music on May 4, 1864, seven months before Fry's death caused by tuberculosis.

BIBLIOGRAPHY

Dwight's Journal of Music 33 (June 28, 1873), 43.

Loggins, Vernon. *Where the Word Ends.* Baton Rouge: Louisiana State University Press, 1958.

Maretzek, Max. *Crotchets and Quavers; or, Revelations of an Opera Manager in America.* New York: S. French, 1855; New York: Da Capo, 1966; New York: Dover Publications, 1968.

Upton, William Treat. *William Henry Fry: American Journalist and Composer-Critic.* New York: Thomas Y. Crowell Co., 1954; New York: Da Capo, 1974.

White, Richard Grant. "Opera in New York: IV," *The Century Magazine* 24:2 (June 1882), 195–210.

Louis Moreau Gottschalk was born on May 8, 1829, in New Orleans and died on Dec. 18, 1869, in Rio de Janeiro. He is important as the first known American composer to use folk-popular elements in classical compositions and the first internationally known American piano virtuoso. He would be worth remembering, however, if he had composed nothing but *The Last Hope* (1854), *The Dying Poet* (ca. 1863–64), and a clutch of other graceful, if perhaps overly facile, salon pieces which were enormously popular in his day and revived to growing interest in the 1930s and 40s.

The American critic and writer W. S. B. Mathews wrote in June 1895 of Gottschalk's work as a whole that with it a "new accent entered into the musical world, an accent distinctly American and personal to Gottschalk" (*Music,* vol. 8, p. 190). The *American Art Journal,* in a posthumous review of Gottschalk's *Notes of a Pianist,* stated that "he stands pre-eminent for originality of thought and expression, and his compositions have a permanence not yet attained by any other native American composer" (vol. 36, no. 6, p. 108). And his admirer Octavia Hensel reported in a published 1877 letter from Austria that Liszt called him the "American Beethoven" (*Home Journal,* Wed., Nov. 28, 1877—article in a Gottschalk scrapbook, Music Division, The New York Public Library).

As the delightful Gottschalk piece in this anthology demonstrates, he utilized rhythms and tunes from not only the United States but also other countries as well—Cuba, Brazil, and Spain, for example. *Souvenir de Porto Rico* is said to be based on a Puerto Rican folk melody or melodies (see Doyle, pp. 146–47).

Gottschalk travelled widely as a piano virtuoso in France and Spain before he returned to America in Jan. 1853 and continued to travel about giving concerts in the Caribbean, Latin America, and in the United States from coast to coast, always alert to an indigenous tune or rhythm he might use in his composing. The results range from the startlingly modern piano piece *Bam-*

Louis Moreau Gottschalk
Caricature which, according to Robert Offergeld, appeared originally in the Buenos Aires monthly *El Mosquito* on Nov. 3, 1867.

BIBLIOGRAPHY

Doyle, John Godfrey. *The Piano Music of Louis Moreau Gottschalk (1829–1869)*. Ph.D. dissertation, New York University, 1960. Ann Arbor, Mich.: University Microfilms, 1966.

Gottschalk, Louis Moreau. *Notes of a Pianist . . . : Preceded by a Short Biographical Sketch with Contemporaneous Criticisms;* ed. by his sister Clara Gottschalk; trans. from the French by Robert E. Peterson. Philadelphia: Lippincott, 1881.

———. ———; ed. with a prelude, a postlude, and explanatory notes, by Jeanne Behrend. New York: Knopf, 1964; New York: Da Capo, 1979.

Root, George F. *The Story of a Musical Life: An Autobiography*. Cincinnati: John Church Co., 1891; New York: Da Capo, 1970.

---

boula (1844–45) and *The Banjo* (ca. 1854–55) to his delightful, Romantic first symphony, *Night in the Tropics* (1859?), which calls for Cuban percussion instruments, and his *Grand Triumphal Fantasy on the Brazilian National Anthem* (1869), a shrewd, technically difficult but rather shallow and pretentious piano piece, in many ways so typical of the hack composers of the day.

Gottschalk was sent by his father from his native New Orleans to study music in Paris in 1842, where his fellow students were the young Georges Bizet and Camille Saint-Saëns. He met many European musical and literary lions of the day, including Hector Berlioz, Frédéric Chopin, and Victor Hugo, and back in the United States he toured Civil War battlefields, performed for President Lincoln, and touted such contemporaries as GEORGE F. ROOT (whom he met while he was in Paris) and STEPHEN FOSTER (whom he probably never met). In New York he knew GEORGE FREDERICK BRISTOW, WILLIAM MASON, GEORGE WILLIAM WARREN, and the talented English-American pianist-composer Richard Hoffman (1831–1909). He toured the Caribbean with the fourteen-year-old Adelina Patti near the end of the 1850s and died in 1869 of peritonitis in Rio de Janeiro. He is buried in Green-Wood Cemetery in Brooklyn, N.Y.

JOHN HENRY HOPKINS, JR. was born in Pittsburgh on Oct. 28, 1820 and died in Troy, N.Y. on Aug. 14, 1891. Although schooled as a lawyer, he was a denominational journalist for most of his life. In Feb. 1853 he founded and edited the Episcopalian *Church Journal* of New York and sold it in Jan. 1868. Hopkins was also a teacher and a clergyman, teaching the son of a Bishop Elliott in Savannah, Ga. (1843) and holding churches in Plattsburgh, N.Y. (1872–76) and in Williamsport, Pa. (1876–87).

While a student at his father's school in Pittsburgh, at the University of Vermont, and at New York's General Theological Seminary, Hopkins displayed a talent for drawing and design. He later designed vestments, stained-glass windows, seals, and various ceremonial objects for the Episcopal Church.

Hopkins' remarkable father, for whom he was named, not only conducted his own school but was a self-styled church composer and cleric (he left the legal profession to be ordained into the Episcopal Church, though unprepared by schooling to do so, eventually being named Bishop of Vermont!).

John Henry Hopkins, Jr. studied harmony, progressing in music further than his father. Besides the Christmas hymn "Three Kings of Orient" ("known everywhere in this country, and England, too," Sweet, p. 68), his biography tells us that he composed "a considerable number of anthems and settings of the Kyrie Eleison" (p. 68). He also set all sections of the Mass and wrote many hymns and carols ("most of them unknown," says the biography on p. 68).

Hopkins, Jr. left many writings, among them *Poems by the Wayside* (New York: J. Pott, 1883). A vivid image of him in the 1850s is given in volume 5 of the Vermont Historical Society's *News and Notes:* it mentions his "beautiful playing on the flute and bugle," his "strange, odd looks, his twinkling eyes, his heavy beard and his extraordinary Byronic collar" (no. 4, p. 27). (It also notes that his family called him Henry.) His younger brother, Charles Jerome Hopkins (1836–1898), was well known as a composer, though he was self-taught, and instituted a system of free singing schools in New York City in 1865.

Hopkins, who became known as "Deacon Hopkins" during his years as editor of the *Church Journal,* dabbled in Episcopal-Church politics and apparently had strong opinions about almost everything. He had a reputation for being disputatious, especially during his editorship. It seems that he was continually embroiled in controversy of some kind. The prominent New Yorker and diarist George Templeton Strong (1820–1875) referred to Hopkins as an "impertinent, self-sufficient, intrusive, low-minded, little busybody of an ecclesiastic" (Strong, vol. IV, p. 144).

When he left Williamsport, Pa. in 1887 at the age of sixty-seven, Hopkins moved back to New York City to accept a lectureship for which he had been announced with the alumni of General Theological Seminary; however, he was not voted into that position. He had to barter part of his library for his rent. Hopkins died at the home of a friend (Dr. E. D. Ferguson), with whom he had stayed for over a year. "Three Kings of Orient" was composed in 1857 and first appeared in Hopkins' book *Carols, Hymns and Songs* (1863).

BIBLIOGRAPHY

Christ-Janer, Albert, Charles W. Hughes, and Carleton Sprague Smith, eds. *American Hymns Old and New.* New York: Columbia University Press, 1980.

The Hymnal 1940 Companion. New York: The Church Pension Fund, 1949.

Strong, George Templeton. *The Diary of George Templeton Strong.* Ed. by Milton Halsey Thomas and Allan Nevins. 4 vols. New York: Macmillan, 1952.

Sweet, Charles F. *A Champion of the Cross.* New York: James Pott & Co., 1894.

SCOTT JOPLIN was born in Texarkana, Tex. on Nov. 24, 1868, it is said (see Haskins, p. 32), and died in New York on Apr. 1, 1917. *Maple Leaf Rag* (1897) "brought its composer almost instant fame [and] made him 'The King of Ragtime Composers'" (Blesh, p. xxi) when it was published on Sept. 18, 1899 (exact date cited in Hamm, p. 395). (A facsimile of the *Maple Leaf Rag* contract dated Aug. 10, 1899 was included in the Sept. 1977 [vol. 9, no. 3] issue of *Rag Times,* published by The Maple Leaf Club of Los Angeles, and may also be seen in *American Music* [vol. 1, no. 1, p. (45)] and in Haskins [second unnumbered page after p. 80].)

Scott Joplin
As pictured on the sheet music
of his *Swipesy* (St. Louis:
John Stark & Son, 1900)

Curiously, the piece has captured the scholarly as well as the popular imagination (Rudi Blesh could write in 1971 that the piece was "still in print and still popular"— Blesh, p. xxxiii). With its brashness, aggressiveness, seemingly *sui generis* quality, and its moments of unexpected rhythmic dislocation, *Maple Leaf Rag* was almost as path-breaking and daring, in its own modest way, as Stravinsky's ballet score *Le Sacre du printemps* was fourteen years later.

Its musical implications really went far beyond "precipitating the worldwide ragtime madness that lasted until the time of Joplin's death" (Lawrence, p. [1]). It was written in a genre that helped revolutionize popular music in the U.S.A. and eventually the world, and it could be pointed to by generations of "serious" composers as a fine example of artistry and musical freedom within a rigid, highly organized structure. (As pointed out by Hamm, p. 392, the overall formal pattern of the piece could be represented by the letters ABBACCDD.)

Just as W. C. Handy did not originate the blues but rather brought the form to broad popular attention for the first time, Joplin not only did not invent ragtime but he had seen six of his pieces published previously, including the wonderful *Original Rags* (1897) brought out in Mar. 1899 by the Kansas City publisher Carl Hoffmann. In fact, all "during the 1890s . . . ragtime (then called 'jig piano') had been heard in the sporting houses of mid-Western and Mississippi Valley towns . . ." (Lawrence, p. [1]). But until men such as William Krell (white), Thomas Turpin (black), Ben Harney (white), and Joplin (black) got it into published form in the latter half of the 90s, ragtime was strictly an aural musical phenomenon that "had come about with the first generation of self-taught black pianists' playing quadrilles and, particularly, improvising piano transcriptions of . . . brass band marches" (Blesh, p. xvi).

Joplin's life and career have been written about in some detail elsewhere, especially by Reed, Lawrence, Blesh, and Haskins, so the briefest of outlines must suffice here: Joplin left Texarkana to wander the region as a musician, arriving in St. Louis by 1890 (see Haskins, p. 76); he formed a band and played at the World's Columbian Exposition (Chicago, 1893); he lived in Sedalia, Mo. from ca. 1894 to ca. 1900, moving in the latter year (or early in 1901) to St. Louis (as had John Stark, publisher of *Maple Leaf Rag*).

The beginning of the new century was important for Joplin, for besides settling temporarily in St. Louis, where he was able to lead a more normal life with royalties from the very successful *Maple Leaf Rag*, he married for the first time (he would do so for a second time ca. 1909; the dates 1907 and 1910 have also been suggested for the second marriage—see Haskins, p. 158). In 1902 Joplin saw published his rag *The Entertainer*, which would become popular in the Joplin "revival" of the 1970s—so popular, in fact, that it perhaps eclipsed *Maple Leaf Rag* in the public's mind as the piece most associated with Joplin's name.

In 1903 he copyrighted his first opera, *A Guest of Honor*, now lost. "A good deal of mystery surrounds Joplin's life between his 1905 departure from St. Louis and his 1907 arrival in New York" (Lawrence, p. [3]), but it included trips to Texarkana, Sedalia, and elsewhere. The piano-vocal score of his now-famous second opera, *Treemonisha*, was probably finished in 1907 (he privately published this in 1911 after no commercial publisher would touch it). *Treemonisha* was not staged during his lifetime.

During his New York years, Joplin composed among other pieces *Sugar Cane* (1908), *Fig Leaf Rag* (1908), *Wall Street Rag* (1909), *Solace* (1909), *Euphonic Sounds* (1909), *Scott Joplin's New Rag* (1912), and *Reflection Rag* (1917). Over fifty piano pieces in all were composed during his rather short career and several indifferent songs (with the exception of two great rag songs: those on *Pine Apple Rag* [1910] and *Maple Leaf Rag* [1904], the latter containing the curious but musically prophetic phrase "I can shake the earth's foundation wid de Maple Leaf Rag").

Joplin died insane at the Manhattan State Hospital. He had repeatedly requested that *Maple Leaf Rag* be performed at his funeral, but his widow did not honor this wish. According to Blesh, she regretted her action for decades (Blesh, p. xxxix).

It is appropriate that *Maple Leaf Rag* was published at the close of the 19th century: its formal outline and harmonies look backward to models in that century and its motion and rhythms look forward to the 20th.

BIBLIOGRAPHY

Blesh, Rudi. "Scott Joplin: Black-American Classicist" in *The Complete Works of Scott Joplin*, ed. by Vera Brodsky Lawrence. New York: The New York Public Library, c1971. (The 4th printing of Apr. 1982 was the first to bear this title; the 2-volume set was originally published with the title *The Collected Works of Scott Joplin*.)

Hamm, Charles. *Music in the New World*. New York: Norton, 1983.

Haskins, James, with Kathleen Benson. *Scott Joplin*. Garden City, N.Y.: Doubleday & Company, 1978.

Lawrence, Vera Brodsky. "Scott Joplin (1868–1917)." Program notes for the concert of Joplin's music given by the Performers' Committee for Twentieth-Century Music, Mar. 15, 1972.

Logan, Rayford W., and Michael R. Winston, eds. *Dictionary of American Negro Biography*. (Specifically the Joplin entry by Lawrence.) New York: Norton, 1982.

Reed, Addison. *The Life and Works of Scott Joplin*. Ph.D. dissertation, University of North Carolina. Ann Arbor, Mich.: University Microfilms, 1973.

BIOGRAPHICAL SKETCHES: MacDowell

EDWARD ALEXANDER MACDOWELL was born on Dec. 18, 1860, in New York and died there on Jan. 23, 1908. Most reference sources state that he was born in 1861, but Arnold Schwab has set the record straight (see his article in the *Musical Quarterly,* cited in the bibliography below). The composer died shortly after his forty-seventh birthday.

In 1876 the talented MacDowell and his friend and former piano teacher Juan Buitrago were taken to Paris by MacDowell's devoted and aggressive mother, Frances (Fanny). MacDowell was taken there to absorb culture in general and to study music. He had piano lessons with LOUIS MOREAU GOTTSCHALK's old teacher Antoine-François Marmontel (1816–1898), then attended music schools both in Paris and, from 1878 to 1880, in Germany, finishing at the Frankfurt Conservatory. By that time he had acquired an apparently impressive technique as a pianist and had begun to compose. After his composition teacher at Frankfurt, Joachim Raff (1822–1882), introduced him to Franz Liszt, his music also began to be published. His international fame had started.

Edward MacDowell
Left, with Templeton Strong (1856–1948);
Wiesbaden, 1888

MacDowell returned home briefly in 1884 to marry Marian Nevins (1857–1956), a former piano pupil of his, and the couple lived for the next four years in Germany. In 1886 he met the expatriate American composer George Templeton Strong, Jr. (1856–1948). Strong would be MacDowell's best friend until the latter's death. During the couple's German years they also met other American composers (who stopped by during European trips), including GEORGE W. CHADWICK and Arthur Foote (1853–1937). The Edward MacDowells lived in Boston between 1888 and 1896, after which they moved to his home town, New York, where he became the first head of Columbia University's music department. He resigned this post in 1904 and died insane after a long mental decline that started in 1905.

Around the turn of the century MacDowell was probably the most internationally famous living American composer. His fame was partly perpetuated and spread by important performers such as Teresa Carreño (1853–1917), the brilliant Venezuelan pianist to whom MRS. H. H. A. BEACH dedicated her piano concerto. Carreño had studied briefly with Gottschalk in the United States and had given a few lessons to MacDowell before his European years. She played compositions by both men at the first meeting of the New York State Music Teachers' Association in Hudson, N.Y., on June 26, 1889 (Gottschalk's *Tremolo* and MacDowell's *Hexentanz*).

MacDowell's op. 47, no. 7, is not his only composition about the sea. The others are "From the Sea," the second of [*Three Choruses for Male Voices*], op. 52 (1896–97), and *Sea Pieces,* op. 55 (1898), a set of eight piano pieces. Op. 47, no. 7 is one of his forty-two songs. It was composed in 1893 (during the Boston years), is a setting of a poem by the American writer William Dean Howells (1837–1920), and is highly regarded. James Huneker (1860–1921), the American critic and writer, thought it was "the strongest song of the sea since Schubert's 'Am Meer' [probably from his *Schwanengesang* of 1828]" (quoted on p. 39 of the MTNA *Studies,* cited in the bibliography); and Henry Finck (1854–1926), the American critic and friend of MacDowell, thought it was not only the best of the composer's songs but the best of all American songs and "one of the best hundred songs ever written the world over" (quoted on the same page of the same *Studies*). Finck also referred to it as a "weird and marvelous tone poem" (p. 115 of the Finck article cited below). The piece is certainly no longer considered "weird" but it *is* appealing, colorful, and emotional—this last characteristic being perhaps unusual in the MacDowell song literature.

BIBLIOGRAPHY

American Art Journal 53:6 (May 25, 1889), 85 [announcement of Carreño's MTNA recital].

Finck, Henry T. "MacDowell's Songs and Piano Pieces." *Musician* 11:3 (Mar. 1906), 115–16.

Lowens, Margery Morgan. "Edward Alexander MacDowell" in *The New Grove Dictionary of Music and Musicians*, XI, 417–21. London: Macmillan Publishers, 1980.

———. *The New York Years of Edward MacDowell*. Ph.D. dissertation, University of Michigan, 1971. Ann Arbor, Mich., and London: University Microfilms International, 1978.

Music Teachers National Association. *Studies in Musical Education, History, and Aesthetics*. Third Series. Papers and Proceedings at Its Thirtieth Annual Meeting ... [Printed in Hartford, Conn., by Cole, Lockwood & Brainard] Published by the Association, 1909.

Schwab, Arnold T. "Edward MacDowell's Birthdate: A Correction." *Musical Quarterly* 61:2 (Apr. 1975), 233–39.

LOWELL MASON was born on Jan. 8, 1792, in Medfield, Mass. and died on Aug. 11, 1872 in Orange, N.J. His influence on church and public-school music was enormous. After much struggle, he introduced the study of music into the Boston public schools (on an experimental basis in 1837, on a regular basis in 1838)—the first time music instruction was part of a public school curriculum. (He was, however, dismissed by the Boston school committee in 1845.) As choir-director, as compiler of tune books, and as hymn-tune writer, he was considered one of the leading church musicians of his day.

To promote music and the Pestalozzian method of music teaching he believed in, Mason founded the Boston Academy of Music in 1833 with the English musician George James Webb (1803–1887). Out of this academy grew the lucrative "conventions" for the training of church and public-school musicians.

At the suggestion of his friend and one-time student GEORGE F. ROOT, Mason moved his activities to New York City in the summer of 1853 and taught at Root's Normal Musical Institute. By Apr. 1, 1855, Mason was permanently settled in Orange, N.J. It was probably due to his presence there that Orange was "one of the few places in the early days [ca. 1855–56] of the [William] Mason-[Theodore] Thomas Quartette that could be depended upon for patronage of Chamber concerts" (Thomas, vol. II, p. 248). (WILLIAM MASON was a son of Lowell Mason.)

Upon Lowell Mason's death, *The New York Times* (Tues., Aug. 13, 1872, p. 5) stated in his obituary that he had "composed some of the most popular of our modern hymns," and twelve years after that the prestigious *American Art Journal* referred to him as "the great American composer" (vol. 34, no. 7, p. 123).

Probably the major portion of Mason's wealth was derived from royalties received from the sale of his hymn and tune books, almost a hundred of them. (William Mason wrote in his autobiography that "one of [Lowell Mason's] collections brought him in over a hundred thousand dollars in royalties"—Mason, *Memories*, p. 6.) The success of the first of them, *The Boston Handel and Haydn Society Collection of Church Music* (1822), figured importantly in bringing Mason to Boston from Savannah, Ga. where he lived between 1812(?) and 1827. In Savannah he was in the dry-goods business; he was a bank teller, organist, and singing teacher. Mason made almost $2,000 from the Handel and Haydn Society collection (Jenks, p. 659). His name never appeared on this collection, and "the omission was ... [Mason's] own suggestion" (Jenks, p. 655). The then-small society decided that if George K. Jackson (1745–1822), the British-born organist of the group, approved of the contents the society would take the financial risk and back the publication. "Mr. Mason gave [Alexander Thayer] an amusing account of his interviews with Dr. Jackson. The doctor, sipping from a bottle of gin, sat and listened to the tunes in regular succession, sometimes interrupting with criticisms and suggestions, which the young man soon found he might adopt or not according to his own judgment, since at the next meeting they were all forgotten by Jackson" (Seward-Thayer, p. 27).

Mason's compilations were mixtures of pieces by foreign composers and his own arrangements and compositions (over 1,500 of them, in all). Among the latter are the hymn tunes *Bethany* ("Nearer My God, to Thee"), *Olivet* ("My Faith Looks Up to Thee"), and the tune known as *Sabbath Morn* and sung to the text beginning "Safely thro' another week" by the English writer John Newton (1725–1807).

The version of the latter hymn reprinted here is from the ninth edition of *The Boston Handel and Haydn Society Collection of Church Music* (1830) and may or may not be Mason's arrangement of a German tune (though, if it is an arrangement, the identity of the original tune is apparently unknown). It would not be unusual if it were an arrangement, however, as Mason very seldom included European material (occasionally small snippets of larger works by Beethoven, Haydn, Mozart, or one of the other well-known European composers) in his collections without altering it to fit a text or arranging it neatly in four parts for group singing. In any case, Mason's popular "Safely thro' Another Week" is typical of his work and the myriad other composers influenced by him whose hymns gradually replaced the earlier, perhaps more distinctive, native productions of William Billings and others. (By the 1820s and 30s, the quirkiness associated with the rhythm and harmony of 18th-century American Protestant hymn and fuguing tunes was largely "out"; the more "correct," if somewhat bland and monotonous, harmonies and rhythms of Mason and his followers were "in.") One should note, however, that in Mason's tune reprinted here the four parts are in open score and the melody is on the tenor line—18th-century hymn practices not yet abandoned then.) Furthermore, its strength and forward motion give it a distinction not shared by many other contemporary products crafted for use in Protestant churches. It has been reprinted in the hymn books of several Protestant denominations, and at the time of this writing, 188 years after Mason's birth, it is considered by many church goers to be an "old favorite."

BIBLIOGRAPHY

The Boston Handel and Haydn Society Collection of Church Music. New York: Da Capo Press, 1973 (*Earlier American Music*, no. 15, ed. by H. Wiley Hitchcock).

Dictionary of American Biography. New York: Charles Scribner's Sons; London: Milford, 1928–37.

Fredericks, Mary. "He Set America Singing." *New Jersey Music and Arts,* Jan. 1952, pp. 3, 4, 22, 23.

Graber, Kenneth. Letter of Sept. 20, 1983 to this author.

Jenks, Francis H. "Lowell Mason." *The New England Magazine* 15:5 (Jan. 1895), 651–67.

Keene, James A. *A History of Music Education in the United States.* Hanover, N.H., and London: University Press of New England, 1982.

Mason, Henry Lowell. *Hymn-Tunes of Lowell Mason: A Bibliography.* Cambridge: Harvard University Press, 1944.

———. *Lowell Mason: An Appreciation of His Life and Work.* The Hymn Society of America, 1941. (The Papers of the Hymn Society, VIII; Carl F. Price, ed.)

Mason, William. *Memories of a Musical Life.* New York: Century Co., 1901; New York: AMS Press, 1970; New York: Da Capo, 1970.

William Mason
At the age of 18 in 1847;
from a daguerreotype as used in his
Memories of a Musical Life (1902)

Seward, Theodore F. *The Educational Work of Dr. Lowell Mason.* [Concludes with *Lowell Mason* by A. W. Thayer.] No publisher, place, or date given. (NYPL has [1879?] for date and its classmark is *MEC (Mason).)

Thomas, Theodore. *A Musical Autobiography.* Ed. by George P. Upton. Chicago: C. McClurg & Co., 1905; New York: Da Capo, 1964; Grosse Pointe, Mich.: Scholarly Press [1974?].

WILLIAM MASON was born on Jan. 24, 1829 in Boston and died on July 14, 1908 in New York. Surely one of the most interesting pieces on him was written by his former piano pupil W. S. B. Mathews in *A Hundred Years of Music in America* while Mason was alive. In it is found the author's somewhat questionable opinion that Mason was the "thoroughly representative American artist, highly popular with musicians everywhere" (p. 640). Less open to question perhaps is his statement that "in his art, work and life, [William Mason] seems to fully exemplify the results which musical culture in America has reached very largely through the labors of Dr. Lowell Mason" (p. 640).

Twenty-two years after he made the above remarks, Mathews commented on the piece *Silver Spring* in a discussion of the distinctiveness of each of Mason's works: he said that Mason composed it "when under the influence of [Ernst] Haberdier [1813–1869], who seemed to have made a great discovery in piano playing in the interlocking passages, which the cadenzas and accompaniments of 'Silver Spring' fully illustrate. This was the end. [Mason] made a great success with the piece, which has been played far and near; but he never wrote another like it, or even remotely resembling it" (Mathews, "American," p. 493).

As William Mason himself tells us in the first sentence of his autobiography (*Memories of a Musical Life*), he was the third son of Lowell and Abigail Mason (yes, *the* LOWELL MASON). The other children (all boys) were Daniel (1), Lowell Mason, Jr. (2), and Henry (4). William also tells us in his autobiography that as a child he "became useful to my father as an accompanist, and when he went to musical conventions he took me along with him, and I would play the piano accompaniments while he conducted" (Mason, *Memories,* p. 11).

He had piano lessons locally (Boston) with Henry Schmidt, and his first concert appearance was at the age of seventeen. Between May 1849 and 1854 he was in Europe, studying with Ignaz Moscheles (along with CHARLES PERKINS) in Leipzig, with Alexander Dreyschock in Prague, and, perhaps of greatest significance to Mason's art, with Franz Liszt in Weimar.

Mason became an intimate in Liszt's circle and met Wagner (about whose music he had mixed feelings). On page 134 of the *Memories*, Mason writes of attending the first Leipzig performance of Wagner's opera *Lohengrin* on Jan. 7, 1854, and that afterward "the whole Liszt party . . . went to supper at the house of the concertmeister. . . . Quite a number of other guests were present. Among them . . . my Boston friends and fellow townsmen Charles C. Perkins and J. C. D. Parker. . . . Brahms also was present, and during the evening he played. . . ." Mason met many of the other European musical "greats," among them Schumann (whose works he later championed in the United States), Berlioz, and Anton Rubinstein.

Upon returning to New York in 1854, William Mason toured only once as a piano virtuoso but, disliking the taste of his audiences and the strictures this profession demanded, he concentrated on local solo appearances, chamber music performances, and teaching. He became famous in these latter pursuits, especially in teaching. He was perhaps the most famous American piano teacher in the United States in the second half of the 19th century.

With the violinist (later conductor) Theodore Thomas (1835–1905), he instituted the Mason–Thomas Quartet which presented a series of chamber-music concerts (patterned after those of Liszt in Weimar) which lasted for thirteen years (1855–68).

After Mason's return from Europe, his parents and his two elder brothers (Daniel and Lowell, Jr., who ran a music publishing business in New York called Mason Brothers) were living in Orange, N.J. on an estate named Silverspring. William named his graceful piano piece, reprinted here, first published in 1856, after their home. (A beautiful description of the spring and the stream that ran through the Lowell Mason property in Orange may be found in Mason, *Lowell,* p. 11.)

William Mason composed about sixty other piano pieces, such as *Monody* (1865) and *Amitié pour amitié* (1851), a *Serenata* for cello and piano (1882), and wrote the books *A Method for the Piano* (1867), *A System for Beginners* (1871), *A System of Technical Exercises . . .* (1878), and best known of all, *Touch and Technic* (1891–92).

Mason knew and admired GOTTSCHALK and helped the composers GEORGE FREDERICK BRISTOW, GEORGE F. ROOT, Henry Holden Huss, and Howard Brockway, but he aggressively promoted only EDWARD MACDOWELL. Shortly after its composition in 1893, MacDowell's first piano sonata, the *Sonata Tragica,* op. 45, was performed by Mason every day one summer at his vacation spot in Appledore, Isles of Shoals, New Hampshire. As a gesture of appreciation, MacDowell dedicated his second piano sonata, *Sonata Eroica,* op. 50 (1895), to Mason.

While the famous educator-composer Daniel Gregory Mason (1873–1953), nephew of William Mason, de-

Lowell Mason's house on the estate in Orange, N.J., known as Silverspring, as pictured in *New England Magazine*, Jan. 1895

scribed his uncle somewhat unflatteringly (saying that he had "the full Mason timidity and naivete" (Mason, *Music,* p. 51) and that he was spoiled, temperamental, humorless, and overly awed by authority), he praised ecstatically William's piano playing and could write this about his performance of *Silver Spring:* "[It] came from his hands as delicate as gossamer. To hear its fluid tones stealing upstairs on a summer morning was to feel a new gusto for living" (Mason, *Music,* p. 50).

BIBLIOGRAPHY

Graber, Kenneth. Letter of Sept. 20, 1983 to this author.

Mason, Daniel Gregory. *Music in My Time and Other Reminiscences.* New York: Macmillan Co., 1938.

Mason, Henry Lowell. *Lowell Mason: An Appreciation of His Life and Work.* The Hymn Society of America, 1941. (The Papers of the Hymn Society, VIII; Carl F. Price, ed.)

Mason, William. *Memories of a Musical Life.* New York: Century Co., 1901; New York: AMS Press, 1970; New York: Da Capo, 1970.

[Mathews, W. S. B.] "American Composers of the First Rank." *Music* 2, Sept. 1892, 491–503.

Mathews, W. S. B. *A Hundred Years of Music in America.* Chicago: Howe, 1889; New York: AMS Press, 1970.

(*Silver Spring* has been recorded at least twice: Society for the Preservation of the American Musical Heritage, MIA-109; New World Records, NW-257.)

JOHN KNOWLES PAINE was born in Portland, Me. on Jan. 9, 1839 and died in Boston on Apr. 25, 1906. The Jan. 8, 1859 issue of *Dwight's Journal of Music* contained the following statement: "We have four American musical students [in Berlin] now. Converse, studying with [Karl August] Haupt [1810–1891], counterpoint and composition. Paine, of Portland, studying the same with organ in addition, all with Haupt—who says his pupil will make a *great* organist; Pease . . . and Pattison . . ." (vol. 14, no. 15, p. 325). Back at home after his studies, Paine found that his country seemed to agree with Haupt: "On his return to America . . . Paine became the leading organist in the United States" (Edwards, p. 123).

After his early years in Portland and his years of study in Berlin (1858–61),* where his teachers were Gustave Teschner (1800–1883) and Wilhelm Wieprecht (1802–1872), as well as Haupt, his years as a young professional musician—organist at New West Church in Boston (1861–64), as low-rank teacher and organist at Harvard University (beginning in 1862), as teacher at the New England Conservatory of Music (beginning in 1867) and Boston University—after all of these, Paine was made a full professor of music at Harvard in the summer of 1875. He was the first to hold such an appointment in an American university.

During these years and beyond, Paine composed much music. (Dartmouth professor Charles Henry Morse [1853–1927], a one-time student of Paine's, echoed the sentiments of much of the musical public of the day when he called Paine "America's greatest composer by far" [Edwards, p. 139].)

While at Harvard, but before he was appointed full professor, Paine composed the large-scale oratorio *St. Peter,* op. 20 (1870–72) on texts selected from the Bible. Schmidt (p. 423) quotes Louis Elson as writing that it was "the first oratorio written on American soil," a claim that is false: it is believed that John Hill Hewitt's *Jeptha* (1845) has that distinction. However, Paine's obituary in *The New York Times* (Apr. 26, 1906, p. 11) was more correct in calling it "his first [major] musical composition produced in his native land."

The well-received première of *St. Peter* was conducted by Paine himself in his home town on June 3, 1873, and featured the Haydn Association with four vocal soloists and the Germania Orchestra. Schmidt writes (p. 425) that the oratorio "shows the strong influence of its models," those of Bach (perhaps Paine's favorite composer at this time) and Mendelssohn (who was a current favorite in the United States).

St. Peter is in two parts: "The Divine Call" (nos. 1–8) and "The Denial and Repentance" (nos. 9–19) form the first; "The Ascension" (nos. 20–26) and "Pentecost" (nos. 27–39) form the second. Reprinted here are no. 34, a recitative for Peter (a bass) and a passage for the twelve disciples (male chorus), and no. 35, a chorus beginning with the words "This the witness of God."

Azara (begun spring 1883, German translation completed by July 1898) was Paine's last completed major work. According to Schmidt it is "the supreme effort of [Paine's] life" (p. 193) and "a summation of his compositional career" (p. 562). Walter Spalding calls it "an important landmark in the history of American music" (p. 155). Despite offers from authors William Dean Howells and Thomas Bailey Aldrich (see Spalding, p. 156), Paine, for better or worse, wrote his own libretto in

---

*The dates in this sketch occasionally conflict with those given in the Paine article in the *Dictionary of American Biography.* The dates in the present sketch are the correct ones.

rhyming verse on *Aucassin and Nicolette*, the 13th-century French fable. By the time he composed *Azara*, Paine had gradually shifted styles from one classically oriented to another more chromatic and "modern," as did other composers who found the works of Liszt and Wagner irresistible.

Though praised by Paine's fellow musicians and friends who saw the manuscript, and mentioned prominently in the press at the time, *Azara* was not staged during Paine's lifetime. Furthermore, it has not been staged as of Jan. 1988, though it was considered by the Metropolitan Opera in 1907 as a vehicle for Emma Calvé (see Cantrell). The libretto was published (Cambridge, Mass.: Printed at the Riverside Press, 1898), the piano-vocal score was published (Leipzig: Breitkopf & Härtel, 1901), the opera's ballet music ("Three Moorish Dances") was published by Breitkopf & Härtel in a piano arrangement, and Paine's widow financed the publication of the full score and thirty-three parts (Breitkopf & Härtel, 1908). So it is not as if the opera's materials were not exposed.

The long, complicated plot of the opera will not be retold here since scores and libretto *have* been published and since it is available in the Schmidt book, in *Famous Composers and Their Works* (Louis C. Elson, ed.; Boston: J. B. Millet & Co., 1909), and in E. E. Hipscher's *American Opera and Its Composers* (Philadelphia: Theodore Presser, 1934; reprinted New York: Da Capo, 1978). Suffice it to say that the plot sticks rather closely to *Aucassin and Nicolette* (with names changed, of course: Nicolette becomes Azara, etc.) and that it abounds in battles, passions, disguises, and love triumphant—all the things so dear to the heart of 19th-century opera. The beautiful encounter between hero and heroine reprinted here is Scene V of Act II.

BIBLIOGRAPHY

Cantrell, Barton. *Guide to Some American Operas 1730–1930.* Unpublished typescript in the Music Division, The New York Public Library.

Edwards, George Thornton. *Music and Musicians of Maine.* Portland, Me.: The Southworth Press, 1928; New York: AMS Press, 1970; New York: Da Capo, 1987.

Schmidt, John C. *The Life and Works of John Knowles Paine.* Ann Arbor, Mich.: UMI Press, 1979, 1980.

Spalding, Walter R. *Music at Harvard.* New York: Coward-McCann, 1935.

John Knowles Paine
Photograph, 1873

ALFRED HUMPHREYS PEASE was born on May 6, 1838 in Cleveland, Ohio and died on July 12, 1882 in St. Louis, Mo. He lived in Berlin between 1857 and 1863, at the same time his more successful countryman JOHN KNOWLES PAINE was there—they both studied orchestration with Wilhelm Wieprecht—though he returned to the United States for a short period during 1860–61. Two of Pease's piano teachers in Berlin were Theodore Kullak (1818–1882) and Hans von Bülow (1830–1894). Prior to his European sojourn Pease attended Kenyon College in Gambier, Ohio for two years, 1855–57.

Pease's parents were opposed to his becoming a professional musician—a risky and unorthodox profession for a man in mid-19th-century America—so he left college and went abroad ostensibly to study painting and drawing. Pease told his parents only a little later of his real intentions, and they apparently became reconciled to the idea.

Pease's American debut recital as a pianist took place in Feb. 1864 (when he was twenty-six years old) at New York's Dodworth Hall. He played two opera transcriptions by Franz Liszt and two pieces by MacDowell's teacher Joachim Raff (1822–1882). Subsequently, his career as a performer in New York and on tour was largely as an assisting pianist with such artists as WILLIAM MASON and accompanist for many others, including the Norwegian violinist Ole Bull (1810–1880) and the Scottish soprano Euphrosyne Parepa-Rosa (1836–1874).

Pease never married, and he died in St. Louis after visiting a friend. Contributing to his death at the age of forty-four was probably the fact that he drank so much. Though the assertion cannot be proved, most sources, including the *Dictionary of American Biography,* routinely state that Pease was an alcoholic, supposedly because of the death of his twenty-six-year-old brother, Arthur (1844–1871), and Arthur's wife in a train accident near New Hamburg, N.Y.

Pease composed probably about one hundred songs (published largely between 1864 and 1882), a few short orchestra works and piano pieces, and, in 1875, a piano concerto in E-flat major. He performed the concerto at the Peabody Conservatory in Feb. 1876 under Asger Hamerik (1843–1923), Lucien Southard's successor there, and at the Centennial Exhibition in Philadelphia in July 1876 under Theodore Thomas. *Dwight's Journal of Music* on Aug. 5, 1876 said that the success of the latter performance was "quite pronounced." The reviewer thought the concerto was a work "of a very high order of merit, very effective, and . . . finely instrumented," though it had "too many octave passages" and that the composer too frequently made "the piano merely the accompanist" (vol. 36, no. 9, p. 280). (On the same concert at the Centennial were works by FRY and PAINE.)

But it is as a song composer that Pease is mainly remembered. Along with JAMES MONROE DEEMS and ASAHEL ABBOTT, Pease was one of no great number of Americans to publish art-like songs (as opposed to minstrel-show tunes and parlor ballads) before the 1880s (actually, for these three composers, before the end of the Civil War years).

There was a somewhat simpler edition of the Pease song "Break, Break, Break" copyrighted by Blodgett and Bradford in 1862, composed by Pease while he was still a student. However, it is the edition copyrighted in 1869 by Wm. A. Pond & Co. that is reproduced here. Other than "Break, Break, Break," Pease set six of Alfred Tennyson's poems: "Ay!" (1872), "Blow, Bugle, Blow" (1864), "Cradle Song" (1867), "In the Valley of Cauteretz" (1865), "The Miller's Daughter" (1865), and "Morning Star" (1873). Pease also composed settings of verses by the American poets Thomas Bailey Aldrich (1836–1907)—"Soldier's Song" (1878), "Good Night" (1866), and "To the Queen's Health" (1878)—and Henry Wadsworth Longfellow (1807–1882)—"Stars of the Summer Night" (1865).

BIBLIOGRAPHY

Dictionary of American Biography. New York: Charles Scribner's Sons; London: Milford, 1928–37.

Rogers, Carl Stanton. *The Songs of Alfred H. Pease (1838–1882).* Unpublished research paper, University of Illinois at Urbana-Champaign, 1980 (School of Music).

CHARLES CALLAHAN PERKINS was born on Mar. 1, 1823 in Boston and died on Aug. 25, 1886 near Windsor, Vt. He was the son of a wealthy Boston merchant, graduated from Harvard in 1843, and was as interested in painting and sculpture as in music. The American journal *Saroni's Musical Times* of Oct. 20, 1849, quoting in translation the *Gazette de la France musicale,* told a somewhat curious story about Perkins. It said that a "Mr. Salvator, a distinguished artist," told Perkins, " 'I will take you to Rome'" where "'you can enjoy all the pleasures of life, and you can teach me music' . . . he began composing and succeeded so well that from *Valse en quadrille, romance en duo, morceau en overture,* he has at last reached the Symphonie" (vol. 1, no. 4, p. 38).

In any case, Perkins did study art and music abroad, and in Rome met the American sculptor Thomas Crawford (1813–1857). At the Leipzig Conservatory he studied, among other things, piano with the famous Ignaz Moscheles (1794–1870); there he was friendly with fellow Americans and Bostonians WILLIAM MASON and James Cutler Dunn Parker (1828–1916). Perkins studied art in Paris, thirty years before MACDOWELL was there, beginning in 1846.

Before he returned to Boston in the fall of 1849 (the same Oct. 20 issue of *Saroni's Musical Times* said that Perkins had "lately returned from Europe"), the wealthy twenty-six-year-old had made his formal debut as a composer at a concert of his works on July 16, 1849, in Paris's Salle Herz. He was also heard as a pianist in this concert.

Of this concert—held outside the normal concert season and during a summer in which Paris was frightened by an epidemic of the Asian cholera—a review in a French newspaper identified by the *Boston Transcript* as the *Illustration of Paris* had stated (in the *Transcript*'s rather strange translation): "It is a young American musician, a composer from Boston, who has procured for us this eccentric surprise. Mr. Charles Perkins invited, some days since, a numerous and elegant company to hear at Herz's, a symphony for full orchestra and some social melodies of his composition." The reviewer went on: "It is the first time, we believe, that a composer of the New World comes to ask from our old Parisian society the sanction of their applause, and a mention in their musical chronicles" (quoted from an unidentified Boston newspaper [*Boston Transcript*] article in the Perkins clipping file in the Music Division of The New York Public Library, hereafter referred to as the Perkins Clipping File). (Nineteen-year-old LOUIS MOREAU GOTTSCHALK had made his formal debut in Paris as a pianist, and only incidentally as a composer, three months earlier on Apr. 17, 1849. Perkins might have heard that recital, or heard of it, and been encouraged by the younger American's success.)

The Paris reviewer also stated that the music had "obtained the most flattering reception from our public" but mentioned the symphony's general lack of originality. The symphonic format was something of a novelty in opera-minded Paris, as can be deduced from the critic's wording in pointing out the features of the symphony that he did like: "We would particularly mention the Andante, which is developed with fulness [sic], and the Scherzos [sic], which, though conceived in the classical proportions peculiar to this style of composition, is marked with a true originality." Four Perkins songs were found to have "personal expression, a vague sentiment and a dreamy harmony which could be found only by a musician born under another sky than that of Europe." A Perkins *Bolero* (the same one reproduced in this anthology?), played with "elegance" by a M. Leon Raynier on an unidentified instrument, was said to be "written in the poetical style of his vocal pieces."

Another Boston newspaper quoted (in translation) Paris's *Gazette de la France musicale* as noting that Perkins cultivated both painting and musical composition. "We think," wrote the *Gazette,* "that if he devotes himself exclusively to the cultivation of melodious thoughts, correct harmonies, and powerful as well as original instrumentation, the United States, and perhaps Europe, will be able to count one composer more" (quoted in the Perkins Clipping File).

Perkins apparently took the *Gazette*'s advice. After he returned home in 1849 he composed further, including a second symphony and a septet (for violin, cello, double bass, flute, clarinet, horn, and piano) and also organized musical events in which he usually performed. His first symphony was performed at least twice; an advertisement preserved in the Perkins Clipping File called it "the first ever written by an American" (an apparently unknowingly false assertion: the first known symphony by a native-born citizen of the United States was composed in the 1830s by Charles Homann, who was active in Philadelphia until 1855; GEORGE FREDERICK BRISTOW's first symphony was composed in 1848).

But a concert of Apr. 1850 in which the symphony and the septet were both performed was something of a disaster, if one believes the roasting they received in New York's *The Message Bird* of May 15, 1850. The reviewer, identified only by the initials F. N. C. (Frederick Nicholls Crouch, composer of the song "Kathleen Mavourneen" [1838]), called Perkins the only composer "of any pretense in these States" and hoped, therefore, that he would "take in good part what is kindly meant and written for his welfare and ultimate success." F. N. C. then proceeded to say at length that both works seemed to be hasty creations and that the young composer needed more and better training. He also thought the orchestra played badly and that not only should a septet not be conducted but that on this occasion the conductor was a talentless "fop."

The second symphony received mixed notices: several from unidentified Boston newspapers are in the Perkins Clipping File. One stated that while it was "more pleasing" than the first symphony and did "credit to the young author" it gave "promise of greater things after a few more years of study and experience."

In 1850–51 Perkins was president and conductor of Boston's Handel and Haydn Society (and president again from 1875 until his death). Then, from Paris on July 7, 1852, LOWELL MASON wrote:

> Mr. C. C. Perkins, of Boston, is here, industriously pursuing a course of scientific study. He has cultivated a taste for the most classic compositions; and his influence upon the Art must be of the highest advantage to American music, and to the progress of music generally in our country. He intends to continue his studies next season in Germany. (Mason, p. 158)

On June 11, 1853 a correspondent wrote in the Boston-based *Dwight's Journal of Music* (operated by John Sullivan Dwight [1813–1893]) that Perkins was pursuing his studies at Leipzig and that the American had composed "another" string quartet (quotation marks mine). In the fall of that year, the London *Athenaeum* wrote that a quartet (the Quartet, op. 8?) by Perkins had been published in Leipzig. (Both the Dwight and the *Athenaeum* articles are quoted in Howard, p. 294.) The op. 8 Quartet, which had been dedicated to James C. D. Parker, was performed in Boston by the Mendelssohn Quintette Club in Dec. 1853. *Dwight's Journal* of Dec. 10,

1853 thought it "certainly a great advance upon his earlier efforts, his two symphonies, for instance. It has more unity and continuity of thought, and much more clear, persistent working through of themes" (vol. 4, no. 10, p. 78).

Perkins was the leader of a group of Bostonians who planned and built the famous Boston Music Hall (it opened Nov. 20, 1852 and was superseded by Symphony Hall in 1900). For it he commissioned his friend Thomas Crawford to sculpt a bronze statue of Beethoven, which, since 1902, has stood in the New England Conservatory of Music.

In June 1855 Perkins married Frances D. Bruen and the couple had three children. At their home, "many concerts and recitals were given," to quote the Perkins article in the *Dictionary of American Biography*.

After 1857 Perkins usually spent his time in art-related non-musical activities. He lectured on art, lived abroad, served thirteen years on a Boston public-school art committee, helped found the Massachusetts Normal Art School (later called the Massachusetts School of Art) and the Museum of Fine Arts, and was president for ten years of the Boston Art Club.

Apparently most of Perkins' musical works were composed in the 1840s and 50s. Since no complete list is available in published research sources to date, at least a partial listing follows. Other than the two symphonies and the septet, none of which was apparently published, his works include a set of seven waltzes for piano entitled *The Midsummer Night's Dream* (Boston: Geo. P. Reed, c1842); the songs performed at his Paris debut and published there with texts in French and English, *Eight Melodies Dedicated to My Sister. Huit Melodies dédiées à ma soeur* (Paris: Chez Brandus & cie [184–]), and four works published in Leipzig by Breitkopf & Härtel: *String Quartet*, op. 8 (1853); *String Quartet*, op. 9; *Erstes* [First] *Trio*, op. 11 (for piano, violin, and cello—1854); and the set of violin and piano pieces from which the *Bolero* is reprinted here, *Pensées musicales*, which, according to the catalog of The New York Public Library, was published in 1855. (The publication dates for the three other Breitkopf & Härtel publications are from the catalog of The Boston Public Library; several Perkins manuscripts are also in the catalog of BPL.)

A set of compositions with the overall title *Five Nocturnes and a Bolero*, for piano, may or may not be by Charles Perkins. A copy of "No. 1" (apparently the first Nocturne) in the Music Division of The New York Public Library bears the composer credit "C. C. Perkins." It was published in Boston by C. J. Chickering, 336 Washington St.; it contains no publication date.

Perkins wrote a number of books on painting and sculpture, information on which may be found in the Perkins article in the *Dictionary of American Biography*.

Before his accidental death at the age of sixty-three (he died in a carriage accident near his son's summer home), Perkins had completed one last musical task: the first three chapters of what would be the first volume of *History of the Handel and Haydn Society of Boston, Massachusetts* (chapters 4 and 5 were written by his friend J. S. Dwight; the first two parts of vol. II by William F. Bradbury [1829–1914]; and the third part of vol. II, which brought the Society to May 1, 1933, by Courtenay Guild [1863–1946]).

Perkins was a significant figure in 19th-century American music, not only as a composer but as an organizer, a performer, and a patron, at a time when few individuals, especially those of the monied class, took the subject very seriously. Yet he is omitted from a number of standard music reference works—all editions of Grove's *Dictionary of Music and Musicians,* for example, and *Musik in Geschichte und Gegenwart*. There is not even an article on him in Grove's *American Supplement* (1920; new ed. 1928) but only a brief biographical sketch in its *Chronological Register 4: 1840–1860* (just before one on ELLSWORTH C. PHELPS).

BIBLIOGRAPHY

Dictionary of American Biography. New York: Charles Scribner's Sons; London: Milford, 1928–37.

Horn, David. *The Literature of American Music in Books and Folk Music Collections: A Fully Annotated Bibliography*. Metuchen, N.J.: Scarecrow Press, 1977.

Howard, John Tasker. *Our American Music*. 3rd ed., rev. and reset. With supplementary chapters by James Lyons. New York: Thomas Y. Crowell Co., c1946, 1954.

Howe, M. A. De Wolfe. *The Boston Symphony 1881–1931*. Rev. and extended in collaboration with John N. Burk. Boston and New York: Houghton Mifflin, 1931.

Mason, Lowell. *Musical Letters from Abroad*. New York: Da Capo, 1967.

The Message Bird, a Literary and Musical Journal, no. 20 (May 15, 1850), 331.

Perkins Clipping File, Music Division, The New York Public Library.

ELLSWORTH C. PHELPS was born on Aug. 11, 1827 apparently in Middletown or Rockfall, Conn. (though his death certificate states simply Massachusetts) and died on Nov. 29, 1913 in Brooklyn, N.Y. A few things about his biography are reported in several sources but many facts and details are wanting. And, as in the confusion over his place of birth, the sources are frequently contradictory. (Certain important sources, such as all editions of Grove's *Dictionary of Music and Musicians,* omit him; Grove's *American Supplement* contains no Phelps article, only a brief mention in its *Chronological Register 4: 1840–1860* [just after CHARLES C. PERKINS], which omits the place and date of his death.) A careful and thorough investigation of Phelps's life and works is yet to be done, and this certainly should take place for, on the evidence of *Annie and I* (c1864) alone, with its gentle drive and delightful syncopations, he was undoubtedly an inventive and masterful—if now shadowy—composer from 19th-century America.

Baker's Biographical Dictionary (New York: Schirmer Books, 1984) states that Phelps "became an organist in New London at the age of 19" and that he "settled in Brooklyn in 1857." His obituaries in 1913 also mention that he had come to Brooklyn fifty-six years earlier (i.e., in 1857), and the composer himself said that he arrived there in 1857 (*The Brooklyn Daily Eagle,* Oct. 26, 1911, p. 8). The first Brooklyn City Directory to list him was published in 1858.

The obituaries claim that upon his retirement in 1900, Phelps had taught music in the public schools for thirty-eight years (which means, of course, that he began teaching in 1862).

His obituary in the Dec. 6, 1913 issue of *Musical America* (vol. 19, no. 5, p. 21) lists five Brooklyn churches in which he was organist. Phelps's *Musical America* obituary also states that he was survived by a widow (Abbie L. M. Phelps, his second wife); a son (Ellsworth Swan Phelps, a flutist, who is mentioned many times by Odell beginning with vol. 10); and a daughter (Laura B. Phelps, a violinist; many listings for her by Odell beginning with vol. 12). Ellsworth Swan Phelps was also a composer, and twenty-three pieces of his, one marked opus 47, were found in The New York Public Library. He was listed for the first time in the Brooklyn City Directory for 1881–82, occupation given simply as "music," address the same as his father. A music conservatory was operated for years from that address (24 Greene Avenue). (Ellsworth C. Phelps's first wife, Annie—apparently the "Annie" of *Annie and I*— died Apr. 14, 1900. He married for the second time during or after his seventy-second year.)

Ellsworth C. Phelps died at the home of his stepdaughter, Mrs. Sarah L. Kinkel, at 419 Westminster Road, where he had lived since about 1905, and was buried in Brooklyn's Green-Wood Cemetery (where GOTTSCHALK is also buried).

Though an unsourced magazine article (probably written about 1892) in the Laura B. Phelps clipping file in the Music Division, The New York Public Library, incorrectly claims that Ellsworth C. Phelps "had the first orchestral work by an American composer performed in this country" (that honor may belong to GEORGE FREDERICK BRISTOW, whose *Concert Overture,* op. 3, was performed by the New York Philharmonic in Jan. 1847), Phelps did have his instrumental and other compositions performed and published with some regularity throughout his lifetime.

In a review of Phelps's *Hiawatha* Symphony (a review undoubtedly written by the explosive composer Charles Jerome Hopkins [1836–1898]—see the biographical sketch here on his brother JOHN HENRY HOPKINS), Phelps is called "one of the best four orchestral writers America has yet produced" (*Philharmonic Journal and Orpheonist,* no. 96 [Apr. 1878], p. 4). (The other three named, incidentally, are PAINE, BUCK, and Otis Boise.) And the periodical *Music* (vol. 2, no. 1, p. 42) refers to Phelps as "the well known American composer."

Phelps was apparently something of a propagandist for the American composer. Certainly he was supportive of American music in general as can be surmised from this quotation from a letter to the *Brooklyn Daily Eagle* (in which he complains about the conductor Theodore Thomas): "As cosmopolitan as Mr. Thomas is in general, is he doing all that he might do for native art[?] It is to be hoped that he will show a more liberal spirit in that direction in the future. The musical art is destined to move forward with everything else, and Mr. Thomas is in a position to aid it if he will. If American composers could have a fair representation of their works, it would doubtless give a great impetus to art" (*The Brooklyn Daily Eagle,* July 24, 1878, p. 3).

The sources that mention Phelps make conflicting claims for him as a composer. Most of the sources mention the *Hiawatha* and *Emancipation* symphonies and *David* (variously called a cantata and an operetta), but there are tempting and mysterious references to other works: one finds mention of "2 comic operas," "4 symphonic poems," "concert overtures," and "more than 200 pieces in all" ("about 500," states his obituary in the *Brooklyn Daily Eagle* of Nov. 30, 1913, p. 4).

Because no reliable list of Phelps's compositions is

Ellsworth C. Phelps
Photograph from his obituary in the
Brooklyn Daily Eagle, Nov. 13, 1913

extant (some of his compositions are not mentioned in any source), and because his manuscripts and copies of his published works seem so fugitive, I will mention here all Phelps titles I have seen references to or have examined (library locations for the latter are given*; there are also occasional quotations from reviews and performance dates when known):

American Legend
For violin and orchestra.
Performed Steinway Hall, N.Y.C., Mar. 30 and 31, 1885.

"Mr. Phelps's 'American Legend,' for violin and orchestra, is no more American than Chinese, but it will pass muster as a bit of smooth cantabile, to which M. [Ovide] Musin's expressive playing lent momentary charm" (*The New York Times*, Mar. 31, 1885, p. 5).
No copy found.

Annie and I
New York: Wm. A. Pond, 1864.
(Described on the title page as a "Sonnet for the Pianoforte.")
7 pp.
DLC; NN

*Library sigla and abbreviations used in this sketch: BRp (Brooklyn Public Library); DLC (Music Division, Library of Congress); NN (The New York Public Library, Music Division, if not stated otherwise); NUC (National Union Catalog/Pre-1956 Imprints); Hipsher (Edward Ellsworth Hipsher, *American Opera and Its Composers*, Philadelphia: Presser, 1927; New York: Da Capo, 1978).

Bamboula Polka; subject partly from Gottschalk . . .
New York: Firth, Pond & Co., 1853.
Piano.
5 pp.
DLC

Columbus
Tone poem for orchestra.
Performed by the Manuscript Society, Carnegie Hall, N.Y.C., Oct. 24, 1895.
No copy found.

Concert Overture
For orchestra.
Performed by the Boston Symphony Orchestra, conducted by Emil Paur, Brooklyn, N.Y., Mar. 27, 1887.
No copy found.

David, the Son of Jesse; or, The Peasant, the Princess and the Prophet
Cantata (or, as the review quoted below describes it, "scriptural operetta") for soloists, chorus, and orchestra.

David . . . A Sacred Operetta, in Two Parts, Libretto by E. S. Brooks. Brooklyn: E. C. Phelps, 1883. [Libretto]
NN: Billy Rose Theatre Collection

David . . . Libretto by E. S. Brooks. . . . Brooklyn: E. C. Phelps, 1883. [Vocal score]
Performed by soloists, chorus of 150, and orchestra conducted by Rafael Navarro, at the Brooklyn Academy of Music, Brooklyn, N.Y., Apr. 16 and May 10, 1883.

"Mr. Phelps is an able composer, and has put some good music into the piece, but the libretto is poor, and there is no action to keep any body awake, and the reprehensible singers employed . . . killed it, I fear" (*American Art Journal*, vol. 39, no. 1 [Apr. 28, 1883], p. 7).
DLC

"Dearest to Thee"
Words by H. S. Cornwell.
New York: Firth, Pond, 1853.
For voice and piano.
5 pp.
NUC

Elegy
For orchestra.
Performed in N.Y.C., Apr. 12, 1886 and in Philadelphia at a meeting of the Music Teachers National Assn. on July 12, 1889. Of the Philadelphia concert, the *American Art Journal* reported that the "thematic development" of Phelps's *Elegy* "is admirable," but that "none of these [American] works had an adequate hearing . . . for the orchestra was one of the most inefficient that we have ever met with at a serious concert" (*American Art Journal*, vol. 53, no. 13 [July 13, 1889], p. 197).

Of this piece the composer noted in 1878: "I find myself scoring an elegy in memory of our [William Cullen] Bryant for grand orchestra, which I hope will prove worthy. . . . The 'Elegy' is an andante in D flat major, entirely free from any funereal suggestions, embodying perhaps something of the

spirit of the last lines of 'Thanatopsis'" (*The Brooklyn Daily Eagle*, July 24, 1878, p. 3).
No copy found.

The Emancipation (Historic Choral Symphony)
For orchestra and chorus.
Performed by soloists, chorus of 150, and an orchestra of sixty conducted by Phelps, at the Academy of Music, Brooklyn, N.Y., Mar. 2, 1880.

In six movements, as follows (with the composer's comments as they appear in the program at NN and in *Dwight's Journal of Music*, vol. 40, no. 1015 [Mar. 27, 1880], p. 48):

1. *Adagio non troppo.* (The long night of bondage. The cries of the oppressed.)
2. Plantation Dances. *Allegro moderato.* (Lights and shadows of slave life. Nothing expresses more distinctly the emotions and characteristics of the African race than these mournful and grotesque rhythms in dance forms.)
3. "The Slave Girl's Dream." *Allegretto.* (In this Rhapsodie I have attempted to depict the unrest and aspirations of a young woman longing for liberty.) [See separate listing under this title.]
4. Conflict. *Allegro agitato.* (This movement portrays the final arbitration by arms. The conflict of the opposing principles of freedom and slavery. In the Finale the death of Lincoln is indicated by a wild episode of universal grief, leading to
5. The Funeral March. *Adagio, con dolore.*
6. "Laus Deo." Whittier's Hymn.
   For contralto solo, chorus, and orchestra.

"In my opinion the author's ability to orchestrate is greater than his capacity to originate. His treatment of the different instruments is really excellent; but he has a tendency to be diffuse and monotonous.... but we all—we Americans— have reason to be thoroughly glad that we have among us men of pluck, energy, and devotion to art, who are surely laying the foundations for the musical eminence which is at some future day to be ours. All honor, then, to Mr. Phelps... and others who have given orchestral form and shape to their musical thoughts and aspirations" (*Dwight's Journal of Music*, vol. 40, no. 1015 [Mar. 27, 1880], p. 48).
No copy found.

The Enchantress
Staged cantata or operetta.
Performed by soloists, a chorus of "about one hundred prettily attired young Misses," and members of the New York Philharmonic conducted by GEORGE FREDERICK BRISTOW and J. M. Hager, at Plymouth Church, Brooklyn, N.Y., June 19, 1860.

"This is altogether the most ambitious musical attempt ever undertaken in our city, and demands more than usual attention from us.... The music... deserves great praise, and we are sorry to add [that] it deserves a far more careful rendition than it secured" (*The Brooklyn Daily Eagle*, Wed., June 20, 1860, p. 13).
No copy found.

"Hiawatha," *Symphony for Grand Orchestra*, op. 31. (1873)
In four movements, as follows: The Peace Pipe, *adagio maestoso, allegro vivace;* Song of Nokomis, *andantino;* Dance of Pan Puk Kemis, *allegro vivace;* Hiawatha's Departure, *allegro molto.*
Autograph manuscript at NN:
(On flyleaf in Phelps's hand [transcribed]: "Played under my direction March 1879; [played under] Thomas direction May 10, 1879 in Philharmonic Society (4th & 5th mvts.); [played under Thomas direction] in Chicago 1889 (2d & 3d mvts.)."

Phelps was most likely mistaken on the flyleaf of the manuscript, writing 1879 instead of 1878; if not, this would mean that there were two documented performances of this symphony, as well as performances of two movements on two other occasions.

After the première performance on Mar. 14, 1878 as the opening concert of Brooklyn's Music Hall, with the Theodore Thomas orchestra conducted by Phelps, the *Brooklyn Daily Eagle* reported: "The new Brooklyn Music Hall, at the intersection of Fulton and Flatbush avenues, was opened to the public last evening... its capacity [is] 1,217." When Phelps, "that Offenbachian person was recognized, [there was] a burst of hearty applause." Phelps preserved "perfect control of the orchestra throughout... the treatment is original.... What Longfellow did in words, Mr. Phelps has accurately done in music.... Mr. Phelps was enthusiastically applauded at the end of each movement, and at the close of the symphony was called upon for a speech. He responded very briefly, thanking orchestra and audience alike for the encouragement they had given him, and hoping that in the future he would be able to do something better..." (*The Brooklyn Daily Eagle*, Fri., Mar. 15, 1878, p. 3).

"Mr. Phelps's work is only for orchestra [as opposed to Robert Stoepel's *Hiawatha*, a cantata], and its production was a genuine triumph.... It is worthy of notice that only two years ago, Mr. Phelps was grossly affronted by Theo. Thomas, who utterly refused to produce this beautiful work *'because it was unworthy'* and quite beneath his notice, then!... Mr. E. C. Phelps has had a rare and deserved victory, and we extend to him our kindest sympathy and congratulations" (*Philharmonic Journal and Orpheonist*, no. 96 [Apr. 1878], p. 4).

"I Heard You Sighing in Your Dream"
Words by H. S. Cornwell.
New York: S. T. Gordon, 1865.
For voice and piano.
5 pp.
NN

Inauguration March
For piano or organ?
Performed Academy of Music, N.Y.C., Apr. 29, 1876.
"beautiful and original..." (*Philharmonic Journal and Orpheonist*, no. 85 [Nov. 1876], p. 5).

"Innisfall"
"Innisfall, a song of Ireland, [the text] composed by Thomas C. Latto, and set to music by E. C. Phelps, has been published by Thurber & Wilson, of this city [Brooklyn].... It is dedicated to the memory of Robert

Emmet" [1778–1803] (*The Brooklyn Daily Eagle*, May 27, 1880, p. 1).

"Jesus Saviour of My Soul," sacred vocal quartet
Brooklyn: J. W. South, Jr., 1867.
For four voices and piano.
5 pp.
NN

Last of the Mohicans
Opera?
(Noted in Hipsher, p. 431)

"Linda's Gone to Baltimore"
Words by H. S. Cornwell.
New York: Firth, Pond & Co., 1853.
For voice and piano; in dialect.
5 pp.
NN

"Lost Isabel, or, By the Lonely River Side"
Words by H. S. Cornwell.
New York: Firth, Pond & Co., 1854.
For voice and piano; the river of the title is the Hudson, so named in the text.
5 pp.
NN

March, "La Fête"
For band.
Performed at a Manuscript Society concert, Manhattan Beach, by Sousa's Band, Aug. 27, 1895.
"Mr. Phelps's March was written especially for this occasion and entirely within ten days, part copying and all. It is a meritorious work" (*American Art Journal*, vol. 65, no. 21 [Aug. 31, 1895], p. 323).

Meditation on Mount Vernon
For orchestra.
Performed Dec. 10, 1890 at a Manuscript Society concert, N.Y.C.; orchestra conducted by Phelps.
(Based on LOWELL MASON's hymn-tune *Mount Vernon*?)
No copy found.

New London Quick Step
Boston: Oliver Ditson, [no date given].
For piano.
3 pp.
NN

"Oh Saw Ye Not My Own True Love"
Words by H. S. Cornwell.
New York: Wm. A. Pond & Co., 1864.
For voice and piano.
5 pp.
NUC

"The Old House by the Hill"
New York: Wm. A. Pond & Co., 1864.
For voice and piano.
5 pp.
NUC

"Overture"
"As early as 1860 I had the presumption to offer an overture to the [Brooklyn] Philharmonic Society" (*The Brooklyn Daily Eagle*, Mar. 27, 1908, p. 12). It was accepted and performed by the society under its then conductor Carl Bergman.
No copy found.
(See also entry for *Winter Melody*.)

"The Slave Girl's Dream," romanza from the Emancipation Symphony
Brooklyn: Frank H. Chandler, 172 Montague Street, 1880.
For piano.
13 pp.
DLC

Sleep on Now, and Take Your Rest
[No place, no date given].
2 pp.
(Listed in BRp card catalog)

The Song-Sheaf; a Collection of Music Arranged in One, Two, Three, and Four Parts: Containing Also a Complete Elementary Course, for Schools, Academies, and the Social Circle, by Ellsworth C. Phelps, and Leroy F. Lewis
At least four editions or printings: New York: Taintor Brothers, Merrill & Co., 1877, 224 pp.; New York: Sheldon & Co., 1896; New York . . . : Butler, Sheldon and Co., 1901, 240 pp.; New York . . . : American Book Company, 1905, 240 pp. (Contains several pieces by Phelps.)
NN

"Star of My Soul," sacred song for mezzo soprano
New York: Hamilton S. Gordon, 1892.
For voice and piano.
NUC

Suite Poétique for Grand Orchestra on Poems of Edgar Allan Poe
For orchestra.
Autograph manuscript at NN

"Surf Echoes"
Words by S. A. Wood.
Brooklyn: Spaulding & Kornder, 487 Fulton St., 1888.
For voice and piano.
5 pp.
NN

Sweet o' the Year
Words by N. G. Cone.
Operetta.
(Listed in NN card catalog)

"Thy Story Bides for Aye"
Hymn: words by Mary Douglas, music by Phelps.
In: *Christmas in Song, Sketch, and Story;* selected by P. McCaskey. New York: Harper & Brothers, 1891.

"The Trees," song and chorus for Arbor-Day
Words and music by E. C. Phelps.
In: *The Brooklyn Daily Eagle*, Apr. 24, 1895, p. 5.
In: *The Song-Sheaf.*

Tribute to Lafayette, march heroic, for grand orchestra
  Autograph manuscript at NN

Tribute to Mr. Robert Graham
  "In 1897 Emil [Paur] gave my 'Tribute to Mr. Robert Graham' (the founder of the Brooklyn Institute)" (*The Brooklyn Daily Eagle*, Mar. 27, 1908, p. 12).
  No copy found.

Winter Melody
  "The [Brooklyn] Philharmonic Society performed two of Mr. Phelps's works at their concerts—first, an Overture, in 1860, and the second, his 'Winter Melody', in 1867" (*The Brooklyn Daily Eagle*, Feb. 11, 1878, p. 3).
  No copy found.

BIBLIOGRAPHY

Boston Symphony Orchestra. *Programs.* Millwood, N.Y.: KTO Microform, 1976.

Brooklyn Daily Times. Mon., Apr. 16, 1900, p. 3. [Annie Phelps's obituary].

Johnson, H. Earle. *First Performances in America to 1900.* Detroit: Information Coordinators for the College Music Society, 1979. (Series: *Bibliographies in American Music*, no. 4.)

———. *Symphony Hall, Boston.* Boston: Little, Brown and Co., 1950; New York: Da Capo, 1979.

Lamers, Claire M. Letter dated May 30, 1984 to this author.

EDWARD EVERETT RICE was born on Dec. 21, 1849, in Brighton, Mass. and died on Nov. 16, 1924 in New York City. Despite its very European description as "opera bouffe" on the title page of the published vocal score (Boston, 1877), *Evangeline* is an American burlesque—the first musical show of a distinctly American character, one with an entirely American score. To be sure, it was inspired by English burlesque—with its topical humor and travesties of popular or classical literature; inspired especially by the English performer Lydia Thomson and a company of high-kicking blondes who opened in the burlesque *Ixion; or, The Man at the Wheel,* in New York in 1868. Lydia and her girls played the lead male characters in order to show off their legs in tights, still a rather daring sight on the New York stage.

Evangeline, which was performed officially for the first time in New York in July 1874, is a wild travesty of Longfellow's narrative poem of the same name (published in 1847). Rice, who was uneducated musically, composed the music and his friend J[ohn] Cheever Goodwin (1850–1912) wrote the lyrics and book which seem to have little resemblance to the original poem.

The lead female actress of the show played Gabriel in tights, a heifer (played by two men in a cow costume) performed a dance, a male comic impersonated the invented female character Catherine, and a mute character named the Lone Fisherman wandered through the action without taking part in it. The show was immensely popular and was revived numerous times into the 20th century. Reporting on a revival in Boston, the snooty but prestigious *American Art Journal* said: "Rice's Evangeline has one fair point, the pile of trunks; one good bit, the heifer; one great feature, the Lone Fisherman. 'The rest is—silence!' As usual it has drawn the public to Hollis Street" (vol. 52, no. 7, p. 99).

Rice was a manager and playwright as well as a composer. His obituary in the *New York Times* (Nov. 17, 1924, p. 19) mentioned that he was sometimes called "the father of burlesque." He had numerous other shows to his credit, including *Hiawatha* (1880)—an unsuccessful sequel to *Evangeline; Pop* (1883); and *Adonis* (1884), but he never again attained the success of *Evangeline.*

"Golden Chains," the excerpt from *Evangeline* reprinted here, is a duet from the first act. It is for the two leads, Evangeline and Gabriel, and so, of course, is intended to be sung by two female voices since Gabriel was a pants role.

BIBLIOGRAPHY

The New York Times. Nov. 20, 1924, p. 23, column 3 [notice regarding Rice's funeral].

Smith, Cecil. *Musical Comedy in America.* New York: Theatre Arts Books, 1950.

THOMAS DARTMOUTH RICE was born on May 20, 1808, in New York City and died there on Sept. 19, 1860. He was apparently a man of many talents—an actor, a singer, a dancer, a playwright, a songwriter—but he was most famous as a blackface performer—one of the earliest. He was apparently an excellent mimic and incorporated black dialect into his act. He was a solo performer for years, perhaps twenty years before the advent of the blackface minstrel shows in the early 1840s. He had a colorful life: he knew the subsequently famous actor Joseph Jefferson (1829–1905), met STEPHEN FOSTER, and reputedly made a fortune touring this country and England. He died alone and poor.

Rice did not compose all of the music of the song "Jim Crow" or even all of its text, but he did put it in the form that is published here. (Toll in *Blacking Up* states that the "Jim Crow" tune is very much like a certain Irish folk song and an English theatre song [p. 27].) Rice certainly was the first to perform the song before an audience and to popularize it widely. He was, in fact, completely identified with it. He originated it around 1828 when he was twenty-five, but when the first printed edition appeared is unknown, though it is believed to have been sometime between 1828 and the early 1830s. The Samuel Carusi edition reprinted here was copyrighted in 1832. Exactly where Rice first performed the song is also unknown, though Louisville, Pittsburgh, and Cincinnati are the most likely cities. Wittke in *Tambo and Bones* believes that Louisville was the scene, however (he also lists many books containing stories of the first performance, p. 24); Chase in *America's Music* also opts for Louisville, indeed does not even mention the other two.

The story goes that while Rice was playing (in blackface) the small part of a field hand, probably in the play *The Rifle*, he interpolated the song between acts. He apparently had witnessed a deformed old black man singing the song and doing a strange jumping dance with it and decided to reproduce the number on stage. He further developed his routine by borrowing the clothes of a black porter named Cuff.

Rice and his dance-song were big hits and he continued to perform it for years on tour in other U.S. cities and in England, adding verses with local topical references wherever he went. He became a beloved figure and was known as "Daddy Rice" or "Jim Crow" Rice. He also later created more of the burlesques or sketches that became famous standards in the blackface minstrel shows, sketches such as *The Black Cupid* and a burlesque of Shakespeare's *Othello*.

The irascible, rough-and-tumble Jim-Crow character, pictured so vividly on the cover of the Carusi edition, became one of the stereotypes of blackface minstrelsy: the ignorant plantation field hand, the tough but merry country bumpkin. The other stereotype is the Zip-Coon figure: the big-city dandy, the elegant snob. (For a discussion of these two types and their real-life models, see Hans Nathan's book *Dan Emmett and the Rise of Early Negro Minstrelsy*, pp. 52–59.)

In modern times the name of the song came to be unpleasant to many, though its modern usage has no literal connection with the original character. However, using an alternate form of the title, by which the song is also known, Sigmund Spaeth did write in his 1948 history of popular music in America that "there is reason to believe that the term which has since labeled the segregation of the Negro had its origin in 'Daddy' Rice's song *Jump Jim Crow*" (p. 71).

BIBLIOGRAPHY

Chase, Gilbert. *America's Music, from the Pilgrims to the Present*. Rev. 2nd ed. New York: McGraw-Hill, 1966.

Nathan, Hans. *Dan Emmett and the Rise of Early Negro Minstrelsy*. Norman: University of Oklahoma Press, 1962, 2nd printing 1977.

Rice, Edward LeRoy. *Monarchs of Minstrelsy, from "Daddy" Rice to Date*. New York: Kenny Publishing Co., 1911.

Spaeth, Sigmund. *A History of Popular Music in America*. New York: Random House, 1948.

Toll, Robert C. *Blacking Up*. New York: Oxford University Press, 1974.

Wittke, Carl. *Tambo and Bones*. Durham, N.C.: Duke University Press, 1930; New York: Greenwood Press, 1968.

GEORGE FREDERICK ROOT was born on Aug. 30, 1820 in Sheffield, Mass. and died on Aug. 6, 1895 in Bailey's Island, Me. Before 1860 he was best known as a teacher of singing and choral conductor in Boston and New York, thereafter as a composer and music publisher in Chicago. He has been characterized by Dena Epstein in her notes for New World Records NW-234 as having a "lack of pretension" and an "intimate knowledge of effective singing." He also apparently had a shrewd knowledge of popular taste, demonstrated by a string of successful vocal compositions, especially his secular cantata *The Flower Queen* (1852), the ballads "Hazel Dell" (1853) and "Rosalie, the Prairie Flower" (1855)—reprinted here—and the Civil War songs "The Battle Cry of Freedom" (1862), "Tramp, Tramp, Tramp" (1864), and "The Vacant Chair" (1861).

The oldest of eight children, Root learned music in the manner of the 18th-century singing school from his family, and then studied with and worked for the Boston musician Artemus Nixon Johnson (1817–1892), beginning in 1838. Soon the young Root was studying voice with the prestigious George James Webb, and was hired by LOWELL MASON as a teacher. Root was profoundly influenced by Mason and his theories. Certainly, as a composer, like the older man, Root composed vocal music (including hymn-tunes such as "The Shining

Shore") that was always "scientifically correct," to use a favorite expression of the time, though very simple, homophonic, and perhaps a little dull. Root also compiled song books and wrote instrumental manuals, over sixty in all.

Regarding his life in the early Boston period, Root wrote in his autobiography of 1891:

> Music was in a very different condition then from what it is now. It was just emerging from the florid but crude melodies and the imperfect harmonies of the older time. Lowell Mason had just commenced what proved to be a revolution . . . [and] those who were early in the field had very great advantage . . . such very moderate players as we were, got on, because our choirs produced the new kind of simple, sweet music that went to the hearts of the people. . . . (Root, pp. 26–27)

Like Mason, Root was resolutely a "people's" composer—a genteel and respectable one, to be sure. In his autobiography, Root wrote with candor: "I am simply one, who, from such resources as he finds within himself, makes music for the people. . . . This, it seems to me, is a thing that a person may do well with some success, without being either a genius or a great composer" (Root, p. 98).

With his innate talent but comparatively little training, Root pioneered the new teaching techniques in New York, where he was music teacher in [the Rev. Jacob] Abbott's School for Young Ladies, Rutgers Female Institute, Miss Haines's School for Young Ladies, the New York Institute for the Blind, and Union Theological Seminary. His first collection of pieces was published as *The Young Ladies' Choir* (New York: Leavitt, Trow & Co., 1846).

Root spent 1850–51 in Paris studying voice and attending concerts (including some by Henrietta Sontag, Pauline Viardot, and Hector Berlioz), though he did not see opera or attend the theatre ("at that time, in the church to which I belonged, it was thought wrong to go to opera or theatrical representations . . ."—Root, p. 63). He also met a fellow-American who was in Paris at this time, LOUIS MOREAU GOTTSCHALK.

From 1853 to 1855, for three months each summer, Root held what he called the Normal Musical Institute for school teachers at Dodworth's Hall on Broadway in New York. At his insistence, he was joined in teaching the teachers the new music and the new teaching methods by Mason—the real daddy of them all—, by William Batchelder Bradbury (1816–1868), and by Thomas Hastings (1784–1872). Despite Root's success as a teacher and composer in New York, he followed his younger brother, Ebenezer Towner Root (1822–1896), to Chicago in 1860 and became part of the music publishing business of Root [for Ebenezer—George Root referred to him as Towner] & Cady [for Chauncey Marvin Cady (1824–1889)], composing new songs for publication and selecting songs by others for publication.

Of the 1850s, in which he first composed songs that might achieve really widespread popularity, Root wrote: "When Stephen C. Foster's wonderful melodies (as I now see them) [and this parenthetical expression suggests that in the 1850s Root did *not* think much of FOSTER's melodies] began to appear, and the famous Christy's Minstrels began to make them known, I 'took a hand in' and wrote a few, but put 'G. Friedrich Wurzel' (the German for Root) to them instead of my own name. 'Hazel Dell' and 'Rosalie, the Prairie Flower' were the best known of those so written" (Root, p. 83).

The latter song, with words by the blind poet Frances (Fanny) Crosby (1820–1915) [though not so credited in the edition reprinted here], is deliberately sad, like so many other popular songs of the time, and vaguely classy: the wild heather of the first verse seems to indicate an English moor rather than an American prairie. (For confirmation of Crosby's authorship, see Crosby, p. 112.) The song was indeed successful: a notice in the *Musical Review and Gazette* of Feb. 6, 1858, some three years after the song's publication, stated that Root had been paid 1,200 dollars for its copyright and that the sheet-music sale of the song "still continues" (vol. 9, no. 3, p. 34). Root's obituary in the *New York Times* (Aug. 8, 1895, p. 2) claimed that the song was "of that sentimental and not too lofty type which pleases the general public," and that "everybody knows the chorus."

BIBLIOGRAPHY

Carder, Polly. Letter of June 1, 1983 to this writer.

Crosby, Fanny. *Memories of Eighty Years*. Boston: James H. Earle and Co., 1906.

Epstein, Dena J. *Music Publishing in Chicago before 1871: The Firm of Root & Cady, 1858–1871*. Detroit: Information Coordinators, 1969.

Root, George Frederick. *The Story of a Musical Life: An Autobiography*. Cincinnati: John Church Co., 1891; New York: Da Capo, 1970.

BIOGRAPHICAL SKETCHES: Shaw

OLIVER SHAW was born on Mar. 13, 1779 in Middleboro, Mass. and died on Dec. 31, 1848 (or Jan. 1, 1849, according to the Providence, R.I. death records) in Providence. By the time he was twenty-one in 1800, Shaw was completely blind. He lost the sight of one eye in a boyhood accident and of the other in nautical activities with his father. At the age of thirty-three in Oct. 1812, he married and subsequently fathered seven children.

After his blindness, Shaw turned to a career in music from his regular one at sea. He became well known as an organist—he held that position in the First Congregational Church of Providence—and composer. His instrumental collection, *For the Gentleman,* was published in 1807. Shaw wrote many hymn-tunes, piano pieces, and songs. He opened a music store in Providence about 1817 from which he issued and sold many of his compositions.

Shaw's popular sacred song "Mary's Tears" (published in 1817) was performed in a concert in Boston on July 5, 1817 by the prestigious choral organization the Handel & Haydn Society, attended by the President of the United States, James Monroe. The song was performed as a solo by Shaw. It was published and thereafter performed frequently in Boston and New York. (The booklet *Memorial of Oliver Shaw* [see the bibliography below] lists 1812 as a composition date for "Mary's Tears," but this is certainly an error as the text was only published about 1816, as discussed below.)

The text of "Mary's Tears," by Thomas Moore (1779–1852), appeared only the year before Shaw's setting was published. It was in the first number of Moore's *A Series of Sacred Songs, Duetts and Trios,* where it was titled by the poem's first phrase, "Were not the sinful Mary's tears," and set for vocal trio with piano accompaniment, the music by the Irish composer John Stevenson (1761–1833), whose general style is echoed by Shaw. Moore's collection was published in the United States (Philadelphia: G. E. Blake, [1817?]) shortly after its initial appearance in England. The original poem consisted of five verses, but Shaw omitted the fourth in his setting.

Forty years after the song was published, *Dwight's Journal of Music* published an interesting letter about Shaw that contained the following passage:

> ["Mary's Tears"] is a composition that has attained for him a mightier tribute of genius than was awarded to him for his [song] . . . "There's nothing true by Heaven."
> (vol. 12, Nov. 7, 1857, p. 255)

And in that same year in the issue of Nov. 13, 1857, the *New York Musical Review and Gazette* claimed that "Mary's Tears" was still "sought for" (vol. 3, no. 12, p. 178).

Shaw was important as one of the first well-known native-born American composers of the 19th century. At a time when U.S. musical life was dominated by such talented immigrants as the Englishmen James Hewitt and Alexander Reinagle, Shaw had a prominent and tenacious career in the years before GEORGE FREDERICK BRISTOW, LOUIS MOREAU GOTTSCHALK, and WILLIAM HENRY FRY came onto the scene.

BIBLIOGRAPHY

Degen, Bruce N. Letter of July 6, 1984 to this author.

Denison, Frederick, Robert A. Stanley, and Edward K. Glezen, eds. *Memorial of Oliver Shaw*. Prepared and published under the auspices of the Rhode Island Veteran Citizens' Historical Association. Providence: J. A. & R. A. Reid, Printers, 1884.

Dictionary of American Biography. New York: Charles Scribner's Sons; London: Milford, 1928–37.

Moore, Thomas. *A Series of Sacred Songs, Duetts and Trios, the Words by Thomas Moore, Esqr., the Music Composed and Selected by Sir John Stevenson, Mus. Doc., and Mr. Moore.* 2 vols. London: J. Power, n.d. (but dedication of vol. I dated 1816, that of vol. II, 1824).

Wolfe, Richard J. *Early American Music Engraving and Printing*. Urbana: University of Illinois Press, 1980.

———. *Secular Music in America, 1801–1825; A Bibliography*. 3 vols. New York: The New York Public Library, 1964.

Oliver Shaw
Photograph, as used in
Memorial of Oliver Shaw
(Providence, 1884)

JOHN PHILIP SOUSA was born on Nov. 6, 1854, in Washington, D.C. and died on Mar. 6, 1932 in Reading, Pa. He was the most famous bandmaster of his day in this country and abroad and his is still probably the name most closely associated with wind-band music the world over.

While he did compose much for band—over one hundred and thirty marches, eleven suites, four overtures—he also composed in other media—fifteen operettas, seventy songs, and dozens of miscellaneous compositions. As a matter of fact, though most famous for his marches as a composer, "if Sousa had not become leader of the U.S. Marine Band ... he probably would have chosen a career in theater music" (Bierley, *Descriptive Catalog*, p. 9). And in Sousa's day the critic W. S. B. Mathews wrote that "Sousa is not a band master, simply, but an excellent and highly gifted musician, with much in him which has yet to come to light" (Mathews, pp. 297–98). Nevertheless, it is as a band man that he is remembered. His entry in the *Dictionary of American Biography* states that Sousa is "to the march what the Viennese, Johann Strauss, was to the waltz."

The man whose *The Stars and Stripes Forever* was to become synonymous with flag-waving American patriotism was born of a Portuguese father and a German mother. With the sounds of Civil War bands ringing in his ears, but trained mainly on the violin, Sousa joined the U.S. Marine Corps at the age of thirteen as an apprentice musician. Thirteen years later, on Oct. 1, 1880, he became conductor of the U.S. Marine Band.

Shockingly, he was the band's first American-born leader. During his twelve-year tenure, he streamlined the band, easing out some of the older, less competent players (mostly Europeans, actually) and recruiting bright young Americans. Writing about these times, he said in a remarkable 1925 article:

> When I was beginning my musical career in Washington back in the seventies, American musicians were almost rarities, and I must confess that the real reason for the beard ... was inspired by a desire to appear foreign so that Americans would take my music seriously. I had the beard when I assumed direction of the United States Marine Band in 1880 at the age of twenty-six, and I sincerely believe that it played its share in my career. I do not recall that the United States Marine Band, when I assumed its direction, had more than half a dozen native Americans.... (Sousa, "Music")

He formed his own band in 1892 upon the offer of manager-impresario David Blakely (1834–1896). It was on shipboard returning to the U.S. from Europe after

John Philip Sousa
Photograph, 1873, as it appeared in the magazine *Musical Courier*, Oct. 18, 1917

learning of Blakely's death that Sousa mentally composed his most famous piece, *The Stars and Stripes Forever*. (However, "some of the melodic lines were conceived while he was still [on land] in Europe"—Bierley, *Descriptive Catalog*, p. 72.) So while Sousa claimed in later years that the march was conceived entirely out of homesickness for the U.S.A., the truth is that it was crystallized at a time of sadness and death on a voyage he himself called "tense" (Sousa, *Marching*, p. 157)—a fact that should help further demolish the idea that a composition necessarily mirrors the mental condition of the composer at the time of writing.

The Stars and Stripes Forever was put on paper on Christmas Day 1896 in New York one month after Sousa docked (Newsom, pp. 106–07). It was copyrighted and published in 1897 by the John Church Co. of Cincinnati. The exact circumstances of the creation of the song version, reprinted here, are unknown, but it is believed that Sousa wrote it in 1898 for that year's band-tour program, which he called *Trooping the Colors*. The song was copyrighted and published by the Church Co. that year (1898).

In an article in the *Saturday Evening Post*, the writer Rufus Jarman claimed that "for forty years [Sousa's] was the most successful band in the history of music. Sousa himself became a millionaire from his concerts and from royalties on marches he wrote. He toured the world once, Europe three [no, four] times and the

United States, Canada and Mexico three dozen times..." (Feb. 14, 1948, p. 62).

Sousa's programming was shrewd and abounded in variety. He was determined, above all, that his audiences be entertained. He brought in beautiful female soloists such as the violinist Maud Powell and the soprano Estelle Liebling to perform with his all-male band. The Sousa programs were swiftly paced with little time between selections. He was a somewhat dramatic figure on the podium with dark uniform and ever-present white kid gloves. He conducted usually in a circular fashion rather than in the more usual angular manner, a technique which led to a bit of confusion in at least one instance. When Claude Debussy heard Sousa conduct ragtime in Paris in 1903 he believed that the use of circular movements must be the only correct way to conduct it. Debussy said charmingly:

> One must have a special gift to conduct this music. Thus M. Sousa beats time in circular motions, mixes an imaginary salad, sweeps away invisible dust, and snatches a butterfly from the bell of a contrabass tuba. (Quoted in Bierley, *Phenomenon*, p. 136)

BIBLIOGRAPHY

Bierley, Paul E. *John Philip Sousa: A Descriptive Catalog of His Works*. Urbana, Chicago, London: University of Illinois Press, 1973; reprinted with additions as *The Works of John Philip Sousa*. Columbus, Ohio: Integrity Press, 1984.

——. *John Philip Sousa: American Phenomenon*. New York: Appleton-Century-Crofts, 1973.

Dictionary of American Biography. New York: Charles Scribner's Sons; London: Milford, 1928–37.

Mathews, W. S. B. "Editorial Bric-a-brac." *Music* 8 (July 1895), 295–306.

Newsom, Jon, ed. *Perspectives on John Philip Sousa*. Washington, D.C.: Library of Congress, Music Division, Research Services, 1983.

Sousa, John Philip. *Marching Along: Recollections of Men, Women, and Music*. Boston: Hale, Cushman & Flint, 1928.

——. "Music Becomes an American Profession." 1925 souvenir program *Sousa and His Band 1892–1925*. [unpaginated]

Lucien H. Southard was born on Feb. 4, 1827 in Sharon, Vt. and died on Jan. 10, 1881 in Augusta, Ga. Like James M. Deems—Southard's contemporary who outlived him by twenty years—he fought in the Union Army in the Civil War. (Southard was wounded in 1865 and discharged shortly thereafter.) The two men knew each other in Baltimore where both were associated with the music conservatory of Peabody Institute in the 1860s and in the 1870s.

Southard spent many years as a student and/or teacher in Nantucket, Hartford, and Boston. He studied music in Italy, and in this country attended Harvard University (where he was a student of John Knowles Paine) and Princeton. Between 1851 and 1858 Southard was supervisor of music in the Boston public schools and teacher of music privately. His graceful song "The Fountain," to a poem by James Russell Lowell, was copyrighted in Boston in 1854.

As a private music teacher and composer in Boston, Southard was in competition with, among others, Harrison Millard (1829–1895). During this period, *Dwight's Journal of Music* said in the May 26, 1855 issue that Southard's book *New Course of Harmony* (1855) could prove to be "the best treatise that exists in English on the subject" (adding quickly, "not taking into account of course the translations from Marx, and the other German theorists"—vol. 7, no. 8, p. 61). For the next two or three years, Southard lived in Norfolk, Va. However, on the verge of the Civil War "he found it convenient to leave that city," reports the Southard article in the *Dictionary of American Biography*, "because of his northern sympathies."

In 1868 Southard was appointed the first director of what was then called the Peabody Academy of Music, a post he resigned on Apr. 20, 1871. Between 1871 and 1876 Southard was in Boston again, participating in the World's Peace Jubilee of 1872 as a choral conductor. His Civil War activity and his purported "northern sympathies" did not prevent him, however, from moving to the South—to Augusta, Ga.—in 1876 as organist of the First Presbyterian Church. He died in Augusta five years later.

As a composer, Southard was active largely between 1850 and 1870. He composed two operas, one in English on Nathaniel Hawthorne's novel *The Scarlet Letter* in 1855 and the other in Italian (*Omano*) on William Beckford's Gothic novel *Vathek* in 1858. He also composed two concert overtures, *Night in the Forest* and *View from the Mountains*, and wrote or compiled a number of music text books and hymn-and-tune collections such as his *The Haydn Collection of Church Music* (1850) and *The Offering* (1866). Southard's obituary in the *Musical Courier* (vol. 8, no. 8, p. 148) reported that "he published about one hundred compositions . . . mainly sacred music" and that he left "many compositions in manuscript." It stated that "nearly all of his organ solos were improvised" and described him as a master of that instrument.

BIBLIOGRAPHY

Dictionary of American Biography. New York: Charles Scribner's Sons; London: Milford, 1928–37.

Dwight's Journal of Music 8:21 (Aug. 25, 1855), 166–67; 12:16 (Jan. 16, 1858), 333–34.

Keefer, Lubov. *Baltimore's Music: The Haven of the American Composer.* Baltimore: Printed by J. H. Furst, 1962.

Robinson, Ray Edwin. *A History of the Peabody Conservatory of Music.* Music Education dissertation, Indiana University, 1969. Ann Arbor, Mich.: University Microfilms, 1969.

GEORGE WILLIAM WARREN was born on Aug. 17, 1828 in Albany, N.Y. and died on Mar. 16, 1902 in New York City. For most of his life, Warren was an organist and/or choir director at Episcopal churches and teacher of music and voice privately, though he did compose numerous hymns, anthems, and piano pieces and like LOWELL MASON in Savannah, Ga. was in business in his early years. In his later years he also taught music at Columbia University.

Warren received a general education at Racine University (Wisconsin), was organist at St. Peter's Church in Albany from 1846 (while he was still a teenager) to 1858, and was organist at St. Paul's Church there between 1858 and 1860. In the latter year he hit the "big time," moving to Brooklyn, N.Y. where he was organist-choirmaster for ten years at the Church of the Holy Trinity.

Warren achieved the pinnacle of his career as organist at New York City's august St. Thomas's Church between 1870 and 1900, the year in which he retired. He died at his home from what his obituary in the *New York Times* on Mar. 17, 1902, p. 9, called "a stroke of apoplexy," five months before his seventy-fourth birthday.

George W. Warren's son, Richard Henry Warren (1859–1933), was also an organist and composer. He was born in Albany and held organist posts at various New York City churches between 1886 and 1905, including St. Bartholomew's (immediately preceding Leopold Stokowski there).

After he moved to Brooklyn in 1860, George William Warren was fairly active on the Brooklyn–New York concert scene, appearing as piano and organ soloist and accompanist in various halls and churches. (Some of his concert activities are mentioned in volumes VII through XI of Odell's *Annals of the New York Stage,* New York: Columbia University Press, 1927–49.)

George William Warren knew GOTTSCHALK well and was billed as the "pianist and composer" at a concert with him on Apr. 7, 1863 (Odell, vol. VII, p. 530). On that occasion Gottschalk and Warren performed Warren's piano composition *The Andes, Marche di bravura (Homage to Church's Picture "The Heart of the Andes")* [1863] in a two-piano arrangement (Minor, p. 385). Warren performed the same piece with Richard Hoffman at a Brooklyn Philharmonic Concert on Dec. 8, 1866 (the orchestra pieces in the concert being conducted by Theodore Thomas) [*Dwight's Journal of Music,* vol. 26, no. 21, p. 376].

Warren met Gottschalk in Albany in Oct. 1855 and arranged a concert for him there the next year, a concert in which Gottschalk performed Chopin, Henselt, Liszt, four pieces by himself, and WILLIAM MASON's *Silver Spring* (which is reproduced in this anthology). Warren wrote a tribute to the Creole pianist-composer in 1870, shortly after the latter's death, in which he stated: "His last picture, sent to me from Rio last summer, is before me as I finish. . . . I look at the dear face which often looked at mine in life . . . while the fingers rolled forth the harmonies" (Hensel, p. 211). On Oct. 3, 1870 Warren was a pallbearer at Gottschalk's New York funeral.

Warren also knew BRISTOW and appeared with him in concert on June 16, 1870 (Odell, vol. VIII, p. 627).

Warren composed (and saw published) in Albany such works as the piano pieces *La Belle Louise* (1851), *La Fête des fées* (1852), *El Cucuyé* (1854), *Will o' the Wisp* (1854—reprinted here), *Bobolink Polka* (1855), *Tam o' Shanter* (1855), and the songs "Rock of Ages" ("as sung in St. Paul's Church, Albany in 1850"—published 1851) and "A Christmas Carol" ("dedicated to the Congregation of St. Paul's Church, Albany"—published 1856).

During his Brooklyn years Warren saw published works such as his religious songs "Hark! The Herald Angels Sing" (1860) and "God My King" (1860), and the piano pieces *Gen. Burnside's Triumphal March* (1862), *Belles of Brooklyn* (1864), and *Caprice quasi polonaise in F Major* (1865).

While at St. Thomas's, Warren composed such works

as *The Magdalene* (published in 1877), the *Second Easter Cantata* (published in 1878), the collection *Hymns and Tunes as Sung at St. Thomas's Church, New York* (published 1888), and the piano piece *Española* (published 1893). Undoubtedly the most famous piece of the St. Thomas years (popular in churches from about 1911 to the present) is Warren's hymn-tune *National Hymn*. He composed it in 1892 to the poem beginning "God of our fathers" by Daniel Crane Roberts (1841–1907), who had written it in 1876 in Brandon, Vt.

BIBLIOGRAPHY

Ellingwood, Leonard. *The History of American Church Music*. New York: Morehouse-Gorham Co., 1953; New York: Da Capo, 1970.

Hensel, Octavia. *Life and Letters of Louis Moreau Gottschalk*. Boston: Oliver Ditson and Co., 1870.

The Hymnal 1940 Companion (3rd rev. ed.). New York: The Church Pension Fund, c1949, c1951.

Minor, Andrew C. *Piano Concerts in New York City 1849–1865*. Unpublished Master's thesis, 1947, University of Michigan.

Who Was Who in America. Vol. 1 (1897–1942) (5th printing). Chicago: Marquis Who's Who, c1943, c1962.

WILLIAM JARVIS WETMORE was born on June 30, 1809 in Winchester, Conn. and died on Nov. 26, 1880 in New York. (His father, Dr. Truman Spencer Wetmore, composed the once-popular hymn-tune *Florida*.) According to Wetmore's obituary in the *New York Times* of Nov. 28, 1880, p. 2, Wetmore "graduated from Yale College as a physician" and "came to this city about 50 years ago." He sold drugs and other medical supplies. The success of "a few sentimental ballads which he wrote and set to pretty tunes"—ballads such as "Away to the Hills" (1839) and "Where Do Fairies Hide Their Heads" (1838), text by Thomas Haynes Bayly—"made him leave medicine and take up music full time." The manager of the Park Theater hired him to "write and arrange orchestra pieces," the obituary tells us, and he "performed similar duties for other places of amusement." The obituary also states that Wetmore's "face was familiar to every music-dealer of the city" and that he was "known and respected by the musicians of the city."

So just the opposite of, say, Albert Schweitzer, Wetmore went from the potentially lucrative field of medicine to the field of music, and he was no great star in the latter field, either, only a journeyman composer and a sort of musical jack-of-all-trades. The book *American Musical Directory, 1861* lists him as "translator of Songs for Music from Foreign Languages" (p. 176), and his death certificate states his occupation as "Prof. of Music."

A few of his musical pieces appeared in the 1850s in at least two New York magazines, *The Message Bird* and *The Musical World and Journal of the Fine Arts*, and three of his prose works appeared in the latter periodical in 1852 (see the bibliography).

Among Wetmore's songs and collections—collections such as *The Oriental: A Collection of Eastern Melodies, Ancient and Traditional, Now Arranged for Christian Service* (1873) and *The Polytechnic* (1872)—is the ballad "Uncle Tom's Cabin" (1852), reproduced here. It was only one of the many musical and literary productions to attempt to cash in on the immense notoriety gusting about the country like a hurricane of Harriet Beecher Stowe's newly published novel of the same name. The text of the song is by Wetmore, too, and it mentions not one character from the Stowe novel.

There are thirty-four Wetmore compositions and arrangements—songs and piano pieces all—not listed in the *National Union Catalog/Pre-1956 Imprints* that are, nevertheless, in the Music Division of The New York Public Library. Among the eighteen entries that *are* listed under his name in the *National Union Catalog/Pre-1956 Imprints* is a distinct curiosity which has been examined. Wetmore's *Gotham Ambrotypes; or, Sketches from Life* (1860) is described on its title page as "a satirical poem in three cantos." So satirical, in fact, that Wetmore published it under the pseudonym W. W. Jarvis. His Preface states that the book was "written some time hence"; its satire is pointed at society in general and specifically at "actors, singers, music-publishers and piano-forte manufacturers." Wetmore might have added composers to his list, for (largely unnamed) they come in for a large share of barbs. Two who *are* named, LOWELL MASON and Thomas Hastings, must have squirmed if they ever read Wetmore's devastating poem.

BIBLIOGRAPHY

American Musical Directory, 1861. New York: T. Hutchinson, 1861; New York: Da Capo, 1987.

Jarvis, George A., and others. *The Jarvis Family; or, Descendants of the First Settlers of the Name in Massachusetts and Long Island. . . .* Hartford: Press of the Case, Lockwood & Brainard Co., 1879.

National Union Catalog/Pre-1956 Imprints. 731 vols. London: Mansell Information/Publishing, 1968–81.

Wetmore, William Jarvis. *Gotham Ambrotypes . . . By W. W. Jarvis [pseud.].* New York: Printed for the Author by C. A. Alvord, 1860.

———. "Sketches of Authors and Music." *The Musical World and Journal of the Fine Arts* 3:17 (May 1, 1852), 255; 18 (May 15, 1852), 285; 20 (June 15, 1852), 332.

Edward L. White was born in Newburyport, Mass. in June 1809(?)—his death certificate states that his supposed age was 41 years, 9 months, and 23 days—and died in Boston on Apr. 2, 1851. On the day before he died, the publisher Oliver Ditson advertised that White's method book *Piano without a Master* (1851) was "this day published" (*Daily Evening Transcript* [Boston], Tues., Apr. 1, 1851, [p. 1]).

In *The Harmonia Sacra* (1851), a religious-music collection that White co-compiled with J. E. Gould, Ditson referred to him as "the late lamented Edward L. White." It went on:

> The well known taste and experience of Mr. White, peculiarly fitted him for the task [of preparing *The Harmonia Sacra*]. The public will decide whether this, his *last* work, adds to his well earned fame or not. All who knew Mr. White loved him. As a musician he was thorough, as a man, courteous, frank, and gentlemanly. . . . (White, *The Harmonia Sacra,* Boston: Ditson, 1851, copyright page)

He has not been widely written about, however. The only substantial paragraph on White in a readily available reference source is in Nathaniel Gould's *Church Music in America* (Boston: A. N. Johnson, 1853; reprinted New York: AMS Press, 1972). In it we are told that White "acquired considerable celebrity as a teacher and author," that "he was cut down in the midst of life and usefulness, and [that] the hands that used to move the keys of the organ and piano so gracefully are stilled and mouldering in the grave" (p. 68). White's death certificate lists his occupation as "Professor of Music." He apparently began teaching in New Bedford, Mass. before moving to Boston.

The National Union Catalog/Pre-1956 Imprints contains eighty-eight entries for White—entries that include his (apparently) best-selling collections that went through more than one edition, *The Boston Melodeon* (1846), *The Cecilian Glee Book* (1850), *The Modern Harp* (1846), *The Sacred Chorus Book* (1849), *The Tyrolien Lyre* (1847), and *The Wreath of School Songs* (1847); entries that include his arrangements (*Verdi's Quick Step* [from Ernani], 1847); his one translation (J. C. F. Schneider's *Treatise on Thorough Bass and Harmony,* 1851); and his original songs and piano pieces ("The Stars Their Early Vigils Keep . . . As sung at the complimentary dinner to Charles Dickens, esq. [Words written by O[liver] W[endell] Holmes," 1842, and *New Bedford Waltz,* no date).

Certainly the most famous piece with which White was associated was the song "The Blue Juniata" (about a river in Pennsylvania). This hit of 1844—words and melody by Marion Dix Sullivan—was prepared with piano accompaniment by White for publication by Ditson.

"The Ocean," White's song reprinted here, was brought out by the publisher George Willig of Philadelphia in 1836. Though not so credited in the original edition, the words were written by Nathaniel Hawthorne. It is not known exactly when he wrote the poem, but according to Nina E. Browne, Hawthorne's bibliographer, the words were first published in two newspapers: the *Salem* (Mass.) *Gazette* of Aug. 26, 1825, where they were signed with the initials C. W., and in the *Garland* (Auburn, N.Y.) of Aug. 1825. They were obviously reprinted later for White simply credits them as "from the Boston Spectator." Hawthorne, who was born in Salem, probably wrote the poem years earlier than 1825, however, for his close friend Horatio Bridge mentioned that Hawthorne did not write poetry after he entered Bowdoin College in the fall of 1821 (he graduated in 1825). In any case, Bridge refers to White's setting and quotes all four verses of the poem, untitled (pp. 36–37). White used only two verses.

BIBLIOGRAPHY

Bridge, Horatio. *Personal Recollections of Nathaniel Hawthorne.* New York: Harper & Brothers Publishers, 1893; New York: Haskell House, 1968.

Browne, Nina E. *A Bibliography of Nathaniel Hawthorne.* Boston and New York: Houghton, Mifflin and Co., 1905; New York: Johnson Reprint, 1968.

Daily Evening Transcript (Boston). Thurs., Apr. 3, 1951, p. 2 [White's death notice].

APPENDICES

Alphabetical Listing of Works with Bibliographical Sources

Allegro de Concert (*Quartette for Saxophones*), by Caryl Florio (pseud. of William James Robjohn)
Unpublished manuscript at NYPL, 1879

Annie and I, by Ellsworth C. Phelps
New York: Wm. A. Pond & Co., 1864

Azara: Act II, Scene V, by John Knowles Paine
Vocal score
Leipzig & New York: Breitkopf & Härtel, 1901. (pp. 223–45)

Bee's Wings & Fish, by Henry Dielman
Baltimore: George Willig, Jr., n.d.

"Bolero"—see *Pensées musicales* (movement VI: "Bolero")

Break, Break, Break, by Alfred H. Pease
New York: William A. Pond & Co., 1869. Words by Alfred Lord Tennyson

Crystal Spring: Tremolo, by Stephen A. Emery
Cleveland: S. Brainard's Sons, "entered . . . 1860 by Russell & Tolman in Clerk's office of the District Court of Mass."

Endymion, by George Henry Curtis
New York: Firth, Pond & Co., 1857. Words by Henry W. Longfellow

Evangeline: "Golden Chains," by Edward E. Rice
Boston: Louis P. Goullaud, 1877. Opera Bouffe. Libretto by J. Cheever Goodwin. (pp. 25–32)

Farewell Ladies
Songs of the Christy Minstrels. New York: Jacques & Brother, 1847

The Fountain, by Lucien H. Southard
Baltimore: J. F. Petri, 1854

"Golden Chains"—see *Evangeline*

Hymn for Whitsunday, by Peter Erben
New York?: Published by Peter Erben, n.d.

Jim Crow
Baltimore: Saml. Carusi, 1832. [caption title; title-page title: James Crow]

Jubilee (*Symphonic Sketches: I*), by George W. Chadwick
New York: G. Schirmer, 1907

Love's Call'd a Dream, by Asahel Abbot
New York: Millet's Music Saloon, 1850

Maple Leaf Rag, by Scott Joplin
Sedalia, Mo.: John Stark & Son, 1899

Mary's Tears, by Oliver Shaw
Providence: The Author [1817]

May I Hope to Call Thee Friend, by James M. Deems
Baltimore: G. Willig, Jr., 1843

Notre-Dame of Paris: Act I, no. 8, by William Henry Fry
A Lyrical Drama in Four Acts. Words by J. R. Fry. Vocal and piano-forte score, with English and Italian words. [n.p.] Privately published, c1864. (pp. 45–56)

The Ocean, by Edward L. White
Philadelphia: George Willig, 1836

Oh! Susanna, by Stephen Foster
New York: C. Holt, Jr., 1848

Ole Dan Tucker
Boston: Geo. P. Reed, 1843. Adapted for the Piano Forte by Thos. Comer

Pensées musicales pour piano et violon, op. 11 (movement VI: "Bolero"), by Charles C. Perkins
Leipzig: Breitkopf & Härtel, 1855

Piano Concerto, op. 45 (last movement: *allegro con scioltezza*), by Amy Marcy Cheney Beach
Boston: Arthur P. Schmidt, 1900. Two-piano score. (pp. 64–87)

Praise Ye the Lord (*Laudate Dominum*), op. 4, no. 1, by Ambrose Davenport
Boston: Henry Tolman & Co., 1866

Quartette for Saxophones—see *Allegro de Concert*

Rip Van Winkle: "Who are all these folks I see?," by George F. Bristow
New York: G. Schirmer, 1882. Grand Romantic Opera, in three acts. Libretto reconstructed by J. W. Shannon. (pp. 268–75)

Rock of Ages, op. 65, no. 3, by Dudley Buck
Episcopal Church Music for Quartet or Chorus Choirs . . . (3rd Series). Boston: Oliver Ditson & Co., 1873

Rosalie, the Prairie Flower, by Wurzel (pseud. of George F. Root)
Boston: Russell & Richardson, 1855

Safely thro' Another Week, by Lowell Mason
The Boston Handel and Haydn Society Collection. 9th ed. Boston: Richardson, Lord, and Holbrook, 1830

St. Peter: nos. 34, 35, by John Knowles Paine
Boston: Oliver Ditson, 1872. (pp. 140–49)

The Sea, op. 47, no. 7, by Edward MacDowell
Leipzig: Breitkopf & Härtel, 1893

Silver Spring, by William Mason
New York: Wm. A. Pond, 1856

Souvenir de Porto Rico, by Louis Moreau Gottschalk
Mainz: B. Schott's Söhne [1859?]

The Stars and Stripes Forever, by John Philip Sousa
Cincinnati: John Church, 1898

Symphonic Sketches—see *Jubilee*

Three Kings of Orient, by John Henry Hopkins
Carols, Hymns, and Songs. 3rd ed. New York: E. and J. B. Young & Co., 1882. (pp. 18–19)

Uncle Tom's Cabin, by W. J. Wetmore
New York: Millet's Music Saloon, 1852

"Who are all these folks I see"—see *Rip Van Winkle*

The Will o' the Wisp, op. 17, by George William Warren
New York: Firth, Pond & Co., 1854

The Wood Pigeon, by George Dutton, Jr.
Boston: G. P. Reed & Co., 1835

Index of Composers

The first page numbers following the birth and death dates refer to biographical sketches; italicized page numbers within parentheses refer to illustrations. Names within parentheses following music titles indicate authors of text.

Abbot(t), Asahel (1805–1889) 291; *Love's Call'd a Dream* (Leeds) 10

Beach, Amy Marcy Cheney (Mrs. H. H. A.) (1867–1944) 292 *(292)*; *Piano Concerto,* op. 45 (last movement: *allegro con scioltezza*) 227

Bristow, George F. (1825–1898) 293 *(294)*; *Rip Van Winkle:* "Who are all these folks I see?" 124

Buck, Dudley (1839–1909) 295 *(295)*; *Rock of Ages,* op. 65, no. 3 (Toplady) 188

Chadwick, George W. (1854–1931) 296; *Jubilee* (Symphonic Sketches: I) 252

Christy, Edwin P. (1815–1862) 297; *Farewell Ladies* 98

Curtis, George Henry (1821–1895) 298; *Endymion* (Longfellow) 162

Davenport, Ambrose (?–1906) 299; *Praise Ye the Lord (Laudate Dominum),* op. 4, no. 1 (Davenport) 166

Deems, James Monroe (1818–1901) 300; *May I Hope to Call Thee Friend* (Deems) 7

Dielman, Henry (1811–1882) 301; *Bee's Wings & Fish* (Dielman) 157

Dutton, George, Jr. (dates unknown) 302; *The Wood Pigeon* 39

Emery, Stephen A. (1841–1891) 302; *Crystal Spring: Tremolo* 60

Emmett, Daniel Decatur (1815–1904) 303; *Ole Dan Tucker* (Emmett) 94

Erben, Peter (ca. 1770–1861) 303; *Hymn for Whitsunday* (Erben) 159

Florio, Caryl (1843–1920) 304 *(304)*; *Allegro de Concert (Quartette for Saxophones)* 202

Foster, Stephen (1826–1864) 306 *(306)*; *Oh! Susanna* (Foster) 102

Fry, William Henry (1813–1864) 307 *(307)*; *Notre-Dame of Paris:* Act I, no. 8 105

Gottschalk, Louis Moreau (1829–1869) 308 *(309)*; *Souvenir de Porto Rico* 49

Hopkins, John Henry, Jr. (1820–1891) 309; *Three Kings of Orient* (Hopkins) 177

APPENDICES

Joplin, Scott (1868–1917) 310 *(310)*; *Maple Leaf Rag* 85

MacDowell, Edward (1860–1908) 312 *(312)*; *The Sea*, op. 47, no. 7 (Howells) 30

Mason, Lowell (1792–1872) 313 *(315)*; *Safely thro' Another Week* (Mason) 161

Mason, William (1829–1908) 314 *(314)*; *Silver Spring* 64

Paine, John Knowles (1839–1906) 316 *(316)*; *Azara*: Act II, Scene V (vocal score) 132; *St. Peter*: nos. 34 and 35 178

Pease, Alfred H. (1838–1882) 317; *Break, Break, Break* (Tennyson) 26

Perkins, Charles C. (1823–1886) 318; *Pensées musicales* (movement VI: "Bolero") 195

Phelps, Ellsworth C. (1827–1913) 321 *(322)*; *Annie and I* 78

Rice, Edward E. (1849–1924) 325; *Evangeline*: "Golden Chains" 117

Rice, Thomas D. (1808–1860) 325; *Jim Crow* (Rice) 91

Robjohn, William James, *see* Florio, Caryl

Root, George F. (1820–1895) 326; *Rosalie, the Prairie Flower* (Crosby) 23

Shaw, Oliver (1779–1848['49?]) 328 *(328)*; *Mary's Tears* (Moore) 3

Sousa, John Philip (1854–1932) 329 *(329)*; *The Stars and Stripes Forever* (Sousa) 32

Southard, Lucien H. (1827–1881) 330; *The Fountain* (Southard) 17

Warren, George William (1828–1902) 331; *The Will o' the Wisp*, op. 17 44

Wetmore, W. J. (1809–1880) 332; *Uncle Tom's Cabin* (Wetmore) 14

White, Edward L. (1809?–1851) 333; *The Ocean* (Hawthorne) 5